LEFT TURN *to the* Promised Land:
One Author's Journey of Writing, Business, and Walking by Faith

BY RACHEL STARR THOMSON

Left Turn to the Promised Land:
One Author's Journey of Writing, Business, and Walking by Faith

Published by Little Dozen Press
Crystal Beach, ON, Canada
littledozen.com

Copyright © 2018 by Rachel Starr Thomson

Visit the author at rachelstarrthomson.com.

Interior and Cover design by Mercy Hope

Lyrics to "Pioneer" by Nancy Honeytree Miller, ©1993 OakTable Publishing, Inc./ASCAP. Used with permission.

Unless otherwise noted, all Scripture quotations are taken from the Holman Christian Standard Bible®, Copyright © 1999, 2000, 2002, 2003, 2009 by Holman Bible Publishers. Used by permission. Holman Christian Standard Bible®, Holman CSB®, and HCSB® are federally registered trademarks of Holman Bible Publishers.

Scriptures marked "NIV" taken from the Holy Bible, NEW INTERNATIONAL VERSION®, NIV® Copyright © 1973, 1978, 1984, 2011 by Biblica, Inc.® Used by permission. All rights reserved worldwide.

All Rights Reserved. This book, or any portion thereof, may not be reproduced or transmitted in any form or by any means, electronic or mechanical, including photocopying, recording, or by an information storage and retrieval system (except by a reviewer, who may quote brief passages in a review or other endorsement, or in a recommendation to be printed in a magazine, newspaper, or on the Internet) without written permission from the publisher.

ISBN: 978-1-927658-48-2

LEFT TURN to the Promised Land

One Author's Journey of Writing, Business, and Walking by Faith

Praise for *Left Turn to the Promised Land*

"Nothing I've ever read about the writing life has ever moved me this deeply. Rachel Starr Thomson shares her agonizingly beautiful journey—just a slice of her lifelong desire to honor God through her writing—revealing so eloquently and simply the struggle all creatives face, year in and out, of trying to balance on the knife's edge a Christian life of faith and trust in God's leading and the striving and pursuit of the calling and dream the Creator has planted in each of our hearts.

Rachel succinctly conveys the doubts, fears, second-guessing, discouragement, overwhelm, and ecstatic joy that is the roller-coaster ride experienced by all who step out in faith to live a productive, successful writing life, attempting to find their way without losing their way.

There is a vast desert to cross before arriving at the Promised Land, but it's a worthy journey and an instructional one that we need to be grateful for. Rachel leads us there in her poignant memoir. If God is calling you to be a writer, or a creative of any kind, take this journey with her. You will not regret a single step."

—**C.S. Lakin**, editor, author of *The Writer's Toolbox* series and over a dozen novels and nonfiction books. LiveWriteThrive.com.

"Rachel's book is a true gift from God. He spoke to me through her story, confirming so many facets of my own calling and journey and His invitation for me into abundance, into Himself. I read, engrossed in her words, and paused to take notes and highlights—whether it was a question, a note, or simply to express how much I loved this book. *Left Turn to the Promised Land* will bless many writers as they view themselves in the mirror of Rachel's story and catch glimpses of God's splendor and lovingkindness along the way."

—**Deanne Welsh**, founder of Unstoppable Writers and author of *When God Calls A Writer: Moving Past Insecurity to Write with Confidence*

"From dead to alive, from editor to professional writer, Rachel shares her personal journey of awakening to her calling. She does so in a way that will inspire you to do the same. This book should be found in the messenger bag of every creative and every Christian. Enjoy!"

—**Kim Fletcher**, life coach and author of *Escape the Mundane*

"You will love this book. It's such an authentic look into the life of a writer and anyone who is willing to pursue the goal you know you were meant to do in the world!"

—**Maryanna Young,** CEO of Connect Ohana and author of *How to Write a Nonfiction Book in 12 Hours, Million Dollar Days,* and *25 Absolutely Essential Things You Need to Know About Writing and Publishing*

"A great combo of both spiritual and practical ideas on following Jesus in today's world, dealing with challenges, and the entrepreneurial journey. Super honest, no hype, but still very faith building. I highly recommend it."

—**Mark Furlong,** pastor, coach, and author of *Prayer for Busy People* and *How to Find a Dream Worth Finding.* Greatestpurposesgreatestlife.com

"Rachel's punchy writing style engages the reader at the very first paragraph. Her colorful descriptions of her real-life journey make you feel like you are right there with her. I love her honesty in depicting her journey toward become a full-time writer, without the sugarcoating or pretense. She says it like it is and gives encouragement to future writers to passionately pursue their craft, no matter the obstacles."

—**Mimika Cooney**, author, speaker, podcaster, and founder of The Worthy Revolution. Mimikacooney.com, Worthyrevolution.com

"If you're looking for a book to embolden you to follow your God-given calling, look no further. Rachel Starr Thomson is a gifted writer, speaker and teacher who has walked the walk and made spreading God's message her life's mission. Her story of faith and following God's call on her life to write, despite myriad obstacles, is sure to inspire anyone who knows that feeling of being pulled to a divine purpose. By staying true to her love, through the desert and the harvest, she forges a path for us to do the same."

—**Kristina Voegele**, author and success coach, creator of the *Writerpreneur Way* GritAndGraceLiving.com

"This is a book about getting back up: in life and business. Rachel has experienced death, impossible seeming circumstances, and doubt. But she never gave up. *Left Turn to the Promised Land* holds so much value because she has distilled down for her readers faith and business lessons that came to her at great personal (and literal) cost. What she has learned over decades of trial and error, and thousands of dollars invested, she now shares freely. Rachel's pioneer spirit and unique determination to not quit short of her promised land paves the way for those dreamers and entrepreneurs journeying to their own."

—**Mercy Hope**, author, speaker, founder and host of FaithTalks.com

"Rachel Starr Thomson is a hero and a trailblazer. I inhaled Left Turn to the Promised Land, propelled not only by Rachel's fine storytelling but by the spirit of possibility she embodies, evident on every page. Writers need mentors, and little-engine-that-could mentors like Rachel are pure gold.

I had no idea when I began calling myself a writer I had entered such a refining process. Rachel's story underscores this, filled as it is with hard-won wisdom laced with honest confessions. Her winsome words in this book remind me to make certain my goals are in harmony with my heart, and then fearlessly prioritize from there."

—**Kit Tosello,** co-author of *50 Shades of Loved;* award-winning blogger at AnotherBrokenHallelujah.com; founder of My Someday Best for moms surrendered to God's new callings after the kids are grown

*"I taught myself to play ...
and I'm not kidding, it was play.
To this day it's still play; that's why it's good.
You keep your nose on the joy trail,
and you reach the world
in a different kind of way."*

—**Buffy Sainte-Marie**

DISCLAIMER(S)

MEMORY IS A LITTLE SLIPPERY. This is a true story, as I remember it, and as my journals and other records testify. But undoubtedly bits of it are not told exactly as they happened, in timing or in perception.

This telling of the story is of course subjective. Some of its spiritual aspects may seem weird to you, especially those parts having to do with hearing, seeing, and feeling things in the Spirit. You can interpret them however you like. I believe in an active spirit world and in the presence of the Holy Spirit guiding and speaking to me. I've tried to capture some of what that feels and looks like to be led on a journey that is frequently unclear or confusing but is valuable nonetheless.

This story chronicles approximately eighteen to twenty months of my life as a mostly full-time writer. It ends on something of a down note—but of course that wasn't the end, and that's the point. Wherever I am at the end of this book is probably not where I am now. You can always check in with me to see how things are going.

My hope in writing all of this down is that you can pick it up, wherever you are on your journey—be that valley depth or mountaintop or trudging up a slope somewhere in between—and find something in it that's useful, or insightful, or just encouraging. We all need someone to come alongside us and say, "Yes, so have I."

If you are in the process of answering a call to be a writer, it is probably changing you. You are almost certainly facing fears or obstacles you didn't dream of when you began. You may be wondering if you are crazy.

So have I.

Is it all worth it?

Yes.

PROLOGUE: STAY TRUE

THE SLIGHT HUM AND RATTLE of a swamp cooler underlies the close summer air in the trailer where I'm leaning toward a computer screen, hands on keyboard. I am seventeen years old. I'm living in a leftover Jesus People commune in the desert east of Los Angeles, and I'm trying to serve God by writing.

Here in the community where I live, "serving God" usually means a different set of activities: more hands-on, less artistic. It means sorting bread and produce and donated clothing, and rationing it out by the banana-box full to a line-up of local ministries every Friday morning and afternoon—a long line of beat-up pickup trucks, station wagons, and little Toyotas that extends all down the driveway and around the back of the property, driven by pastors and immigrants and people who care. Most of the cars are decades old, dusty, and surprisingly unrusted, this being the desert and too dry for rust.

Here, "serving God" means praying deliverance over people who fall on the floor under the influence of the Holy Spirit and then arise transformed, overnight, some forever. It means traveling to inner-city churches and skid row, to struggling immigrant communities and foster homes, and just trying to share the light. We feed fifteen thousand people every week out of our little collection of trailers and one small house parked on a few acres in the middle of nowhere, California. We do it all on faith and don't so much as send out a newsletter about it.

Our mission comes from a chapter in the Old Testament book of Isaiah.

> If thou draw out thy soul to the hungry, and satisfy the afflicted soul; then shall thy light rise in obscurity, and thy darkness be as the noon day: and the Lord shall guide thee continually, and satisfy thy soul in drought, and make fat thy bones: and thou shalt be like a watered garden, and like a spring of water, whose waters fail not.

I joined the ranks three years ago, when I was fourteen, and since then I've done it all. I'm a bread-box sorter extraordinaire; I've sat and talked with cocaine addicts on skid row. I've spent weeks on Native reservations and learned from Navajos and Hopis and Cahuillas and Cocopahs. I've preached with a translator and I speak in tongues and I lead worship sometimes. When we gather to worship, we come together in the heat at the end of the day and split heaven open while swamp coolers and air conditioners rumble beneath the sound of our praise.

But also, I have this knack for writing.

It's 1999, and I like to write with music in the background, so I put on a CD. *All That I Am* by Annie Herring. It's not mine. It belongs to the friend who commissioned me to stop handing out bread and eggs and sit alone in a trailer and write instead. She thought we could use it as a soundtrack for the movie we dream of making out of my words.

I am too young, at seventeen, to see the patterns—the ways past and future are converging here and now.

I don't know that Annie Herring came out of the same Jesus People movement that birthed this place that I love, and that the movement's ethos will shape my life for years to come. I don't know that writing isn't just a side trail for me. I don't know how much it matters.

And I don't know the twists in the road that are just ahead. I don't know that I'm going to leave this place, or that it's going to be deeply wounded by divisions and splits between people I love. I don't know that I'm going to lose my way and feel forgotten by God; that I'm going to consider myself disqualified from full-time service.

I have no idea how far away the promised land is.

I've just been asked to try to write a screenplay that will tell the story of this place and the people who founded it. And I want to serve.

So I write, out of the heat of the day, tucked away in the dim living room of a trailer with the words of Annie's song "Stay True" playing behind me.

Stay true.
Stay true to your love.

PART 1:

Glimpses from the Wilderness

IN BETWEEN

I WRITE FOR YEARS.
Whole books. Novels. Essays on faith that I email out to a couple hundred people.
Not because I see much value in the writing.
Just because it's there, it's a gift, I feel like I should use it.

And slowly, it's becoming a way to express some of what I feel, about God and self and people, and to sketch out how my faith looks on the inside.

There is a day, long about 2005, when I discover a website called Lulu. They print books—on demand. You just upload your files and order a book and you're published.

It looks like fun. So I compile a few of my faith essays, a short series on the Lord's Prayer, and I find a photo for a cover and I make a book.

Just for me, really.

There is another day, long about 2006, when I discover a website called Smashwords where you can upload a Word doc and it will make a new thing called an ebook. And you're published! So I do it. For fun. I pull one of my earlier novels, *Worlds Unseen*, out of a drawer and I upload it. I make it free.

And more or less forget about it.

Meanwhile, the cultural and technical revolution that is the Amazon Kindle happens. But I'm not paying attention. Ebooks rapidly begin to overtake paper books in numbers sold; the Kindle seems to awaken a whole new generation of readers, or at least to do a better job of supplying the old generation. Ebooks cut out a lot of time, a lot of middle men. They change the economics and the experience of publishing and consuming; of buying books and of reading them.

One day I check on *Worlds Unseen* and find out that while I wasn't paying attention, it's been downloaded 25,000 times.

THE LULL

WHEN I'M TWENTY-ONE I decide I need to make a living. I take an office job for two weeks. Exactly long enough to finish out my two weeks' notice, which I give the day before I start, having realized my acceptance of the job was a terrible error.

(If you look up my Myers-Briggs personality type, the description basically just says, "You should never have a job.")

("Be a writer instead.")

("Or freelance.")

I want to write, but I don't really believe you can make a living at that. I figure I can help other people improve their books. I've only read hundreds and hundreds. I know what good writing looks and feels like. Plus, years ago my dad bought me a subscription to *Writer's Digest.*

So I learned how to explain good writing too. It's something of a different skill.

I put up a website (this is how you create a business out of thin air, I've discovered) and I start to seek out editing clients.

Before too long I find a position as a writing coach for a company called Write at Home, teaching high schoolers to write. They require a college degree, but I show them my writing instead, and I'm in.

Within two years I'm their top coach. I have sixty-five students and process sixty-five papers a week.

I still write my own stuff.

But it's getting a little harder.

It's not easy to switch from "analyze writing" to "be creative."

And I'm courting carpal tunnel.

Meanwhile I take editing clients too, doing content and copyediting for whole books. After four years I transition into editing full-time and say good-bye to my coaching position. It's a risk, but the potential money is much better.

It works. Suddenly I'm making a good living.

But also, it's hard to switch from editing to writing.

From seeing problems and solutions in an existing manuscript to creating things. Out of thin air.

I pretty much stop writing.

After all, writing was never that important to me. Was it? It wasn't a calling, just a … thing I did.

I come back and attempt it now and again. But there's nothing. I can't hold a story in my mind. Can't go into that creating place. I can write words, but they don't have life in them.

I genuinely wonder if that's okay. If the season in which I was a writer is just over. I don't have to write … do I? I can edit, make a good living, be comfortable. Get better at handling time and scale the money up even more. It's work I enjoy. Worthwhile work—helping others tell their stories, hone their messages. I'm good at it.

Even unusually gifted at it.

But.

It's not creating.

And I have this gift. This knack. For writing.

To some degree, it seems like that should matter.

ONE WORD AT A TIME

AS I MENTIONED, *Worlds Unseen* was downloaded 25,000 times while I wasn't looking. So I pull my act together a tiny bit and publish it on Kindle, finally, and its sequels too. And they sell a little bit. I get a check for $287.88, US dollars. I take a picture of it.

Maybe it's the beginning of great things.

It's nagging at me that I don't write anymore.

It's nagging at me that I'm blocked. That writer's block, which I don't even really believe in, is stopping me.

There's a guy online who says if you just show up and publish books on Amazon, your sales will compound with every book you put out and voila, glory and riches.

I have a lot of books in drawers, the remnants of the years when I did write. Nine novels, plus I can make books out of my faith essays.

So I start publishing. Circa 2011. I hire a cover designer. I hire a proofreader. I spend a few thousand dollars all told. I publish all year and into 2012 and push into 2013. I get all my novels into the Kindle store, plus I publish essays and short stories as shorter ebooks.

And I decide to take three months off editing and become a writer again.

I'll write a new novel. I call it *Exile*. Beginning of The Oneness Cycle.

But I don't know what it's about. I can't hold a story in my head. I can barely write a scene.

It's hard. Painful. But I push the book out. One word, one sentence, one paragraph at a time. I never know where I'm going. I'm writing into the dark, from the first few words—*"There's someone in the net—Tyler, haul the net in!"*— to "The End."

And then I do the same for the next one. And the rest of the series.

In the meantime, my three months go down the toilet. Life goes haywire. Friends in crisis. Relationships suddenly falling apart. I spend all three months trying to pick up personal pieces and stitch my soul back together. In the end I'm writing in the mornings before I go back to editing, and I haven't made money from any of those books I published and all of this is going nowhere.

I write five books and publish them and I still have writer's block.

I start to write a sixth.

But I'm beginning to conclude that the experiment has failed, and I ought to give up.

I ONLY WANNA BE A PROPHET

"GOD," I PRAY as I near the end of *Abaddon's Eve*, book 6 of a two-year attempt to overcome writer's block (still unsuccessful, not in terms of what I've been able to produce but in terms of how the experience has been for me), "I don't want to write stories just to write stories or to make money. There are easier ways to do that, and I don't care about fiction for its own sake. I used to, maybe, but not anymore. I only want to do this if I can be a prophet. If I can write stories that are words from you to your people."

THE STRANGEST MOMENT

DURING ALL THIS PUSH-AND-PULL between editing and writing, trying and failing to overcome writer's block, loving and loathing the whole publishing thing, I serve as a judge for The Christy Awards.

The Christys are the most prestigious award given for Christian fiction, and winners are announced at a fancy gala dinner at the annual trade show of the Christian Book Association. I'm interested in this industry I freelance in, and I have a friend who interviews Christian authors and musicians as an unpaid side gig. I sponsor her to go to the trade show as media, and I go as an editor, and since I get to bring a friend to the dinner and my media friend doesn't really care about fancy awards, I convince my fellow editor friend Kit Tosello that she should attend with me.

(It doesn't take much convincing.)

The awards dinner at the Hilton Atlanta is a bastion of traditional publishing, attended by traditionally published authors and the host of editors (senior, acquisitions, content, copy) and other publishing professionals who team up with them. Well represented: Thomas Nelson, Zondervan, HarperCollins, Bethany House.

I am a rebellious, renegade indie publisher of the new digital age, so I sneak in feeling like Benedict Arnold and make Kit promise she won't tell anyone about all my books because it won't make me popular. Besides which, it's not like they're selling. It's a little embarrassing to have a huge backlist in print and no sales.

A little embarrassing and a lot too much explaining to do.

Note: Earlier at the trade show I met Janette Oke and she told me to get a real publisher, dear.

We're seated at a big round, cloth-covered table, with fancy place settings and little coffee cups. Dinner is catered chicken.

Anyway, the awards dinner gets underway and deserving people win, and our table gets talking about all kinds of interesting things. The story behind the books; the writers; the challenges of being a creative in this rapidly shifting day and age. At our table are a couple of bestselling authors, an agent, an acquisitions editor, some senior manager types.

Then suddenly, without much explanation, they're talking indie stuff. Print-on-Demand printers and self-publishing novellas to build interest and an audience; the challenges of getting into a really new world. And Kit, who is beaming with pride, breaks my strict rule and tells everyone that I do that stuff.

All eyes on me, I explain what I do. Yes, I print my own books. With Lightning Source, mm-hmm. Yes, I self-publish and I'm (very slowly, admittedly) growing my readership and my backlist.

I admit I've been doing this since before the Kindle. Since the first decade of the twenty-first century.

They ask questions. They lean in and listen. And then comes the most surreal, the weirdest moment of my life:

This table of traditional publishing icons raise their coffee cups and propose a toast—to me, as a pioneer in this new world.

Kit still tells people that story.

TWELVE MINUTES

I DIE IN A PARKING LOT on September 19, 2014, and stay dead for twelve minutes. I am thirty-one years old.

Unfortunately I don't have any visions.

Cause of death: sudden cardiac arrest. Totally unexplained. Cause of living again: intervention, divine and human.

I had decided to go shopping with my sister Becky. I remember very little else about that day, and I might not remember that much except I was told about it, and obviously there was some reason I was in that parking lot. Logic helps some with recall. ("Why am I in a hospital? Why are people leaving breathless messages on my Facebook wall declaring they're glad I'm alive? Why is my friend Mercy flying in from North Carolina when she was just here for a visit a few weeks ago?")

We were going to Canadian Tire, which is like Home

Depot but more Canadian and with an auto shop. As soon as we got out of the car, my heart stopped and I collapsed on the pavement. As that was happening, a cardiac nurse pulled into the parking lot for, she says, no reason; she was just driving past and felt compelled to pull in. She yelled out to my sister, left her car running, and started CPR. Then I'm told a Canadian Tire employee came running out and helped, and between the two of them they kept oxygen flowing to my brain until the ambulance arrived, defibrillated twice, and twelve minutes after my heart stopped, it started again.

My medical report says "Sudden Cardiac Death," which is a weird thing to read about yourself.

I wake up in the hospital the next day confused but helped out some by logic and by the ability to read, over and over again, all the stuff people were writing on my Facebook wall. Some of my sisters wrote fairly detailed prayer requests telling what happened, so I read those until I can remember what they say.

People claim that close calls crystallize and clarify your life, and people often talk about the things they realize they need to change—the big, radical realizations that they've been missing something. I don't really experience that. I feel flooded with grace and the nearness of God. Mostly I feel affirmed that I *haven't* missed it; that following Jesus has been and will continue to be worth it.

But I do get some clarity: I decide that I need to start teaching the Bible. I don't see it now, but that realization will lead to another: that the time I spend creating things, teaching things, *communicating things* has a special value to it, and the time to create, teach, and communicate is not infinite. In my writing, then, is the seed of a calling.

10,000 READERS AND THE NOVEMBER I HAD NO WORK

I AM REALLY TIRED AFTER DEATH.

I live in the hospital the rest of September and into October. When I come home to my parents' house, with the all-clear for heart disease—or any other heart condition; I am officially a mystery—and an implanted pacemaker/Internal Cardiac Defibrillator "just in case," I lack energy for a long time. I sleep a lot of hours and struggle to hold my focus on anything. My old ability to edit for six or seven hours at a stretch is waning.

I welcome the rest and trust my finances to Jesus.

By November, though, I am starting to feel concerned. Sometimes. Freaked out at others. Because once I do manage to get back to work, work doesn't come.

I am a freelancer, and I've been doing feast-and-famine patterns for years, but this is extreme, and I'm older than I used to be. I live in a bedroom with some relatives near Niagara Falls, where I co-direct a traveling ministry, so my life isn't high on expenses. But nevertheless I do have some bills, and what started as three or four weeks off work because of hospitalization is turning into months.

And now I want to work, but the work isn't there.

One day, in a fit of frustration, I revisit my books.

My writing.

After the spurt of publishing for the last few years, and the push to write for the last two, I have nearly thirty titles on Amazon and elsewhere. Some are short stories; some are short collections of essays; but still … thirty titles. And they don't really earn me money (certainly not anything close to what I've spent on them, for cover art and proofreading and design).

I've told myself there's no market for them, or this kind of publishing just doesn't work, or it doesn't matter … it's just a hobby anyway.

But one night in November as I look again at all the work that isn't coming in, and I realize how dependent I am on other people to need me, to hire me, and to pay me on time, I reach a sudden tipping point, born out of frustration and epiphanic fear.

Self-publishing DOES work. I know it does. Other people do it!

I've read about it, I've heard about their successes.

It can be done.

I just don't know how.

For years I've said "I don't market." I write. I don't market, I don't sell books, that's not my thing. I don't like it, don't want to, it doesn't work for me, I don't care.

Right now I'm realizing what a dead-end that kind of thinking is. Like looking down the road at somewhere I really want to go and just telling myself I don't want to go there because "I don't walk."

Or "walking doesn't work."

It works for other people, obviously.

I have *thirty books*. There is no reason in the world they shouldn't earn money for me.

It does work. I just don't know how do it.

But I can learn.

I'm proactive when I'm motivated, when there is no client work for me to do, when I am bored. I am still largely stuck on my mother's couch due to lack of energy (and the cold outside), and the Internet lies at my fingertips. I've read and taken the advice of people who said you don't have to market; just keep writing more books and they'll catch on. Done that, and it didn't work. But there must be another way to the goal. I recall the name of someone who seems to be successful indie publishing and Google her. Before long I'm on her website, reading advice, and then I come across a three-video workshop from some English guy I've never heard of.

His name is Nick Stephenson. He has a course called Your *First 10,000 Readers.* He's funny, and he seems smart, and his sales charts are exactly what I wish mine looked like.

If mine looked like that, in fact, it would change a lot of things about my life.

I watch the free workshop, I like it, and when Nick pitches his full, premium training course at the end—for $997 US dollars—I buy it.

I, who have no foreseeable income and a dwindling savings account. Because for the first time, I've realized something ought to change. That seed planted after the cardiac arrest, the one that says *communication and creativity are important, and I should prioritize them,* is making me realize I need to quit playing at all this. My traditional dollars-for-hours way of earning a living doesn't really allow me to focus on writing or growing a business as a writer, but maybe this is the way to change it.

I start watching Nick's videos right away. They're good. They lay out a roadmap for reaching new readers and building your audience—which, as it turns out, is the real key to success as an author or any type of creative, really—then leveling the whole thing up until you're not just making pocket money anymore and you can maybe even build a career.

I'm fairly sure I can do this.

A couple of the changes he suggests are easy and quick to make, so I implement them.

Then I get an email from someone needing an editor for a large job—proofreading an entire history curriculum—and before you know it, I'm off and running with client work again.

The changes I implemented from Nick's course do move the needle. A very tiny bit.

But I'm busy, and I don't implement any more.

MEANWHILE

MY HEART, which is a little scarred from all the defibrillating, is behaving okay these days. But I don't really feel … well. My energy isn't fully back. I'm still struggling to focus. And I'm starting to notice swelling in my abdomen that was never there before.

I figure I just had a cardiac arrest; that's bound to change some things in your body. Besides, I'm in my thirties now and everyone says your hormones change.

So I ignore it.

PART 2:

Abba's Ford

YOU'RE NOT IN THE WILDERNESS ANYMORE

IT'S SPRING IN BRITISH COLUMBIA, on Canada's rainy, green-and-grey west coast, and I am up at 5 a.m., meditating on the carpeted floor of Nina's basement.

Nina Redline is a friend, a new friend, with a basement suite where I'm living for a few months.

It went like this: I went out for coffee with Carolyn, who is my roommate, my ministry partner, and one of my best friends. We've been doing ministry together since 2007 and recently changed our name, from Soli Deo Gloria Ballet to 1:11 Ministries. Our planning sessions are typically pretty simple.

We plunked ourselves down at Tim Horton's with our respective coffee and chai tea with cream, and Carolyn said, "So where do we want to tour next?"

And I'm not even sure I'd really thought about it, but it just came out of my mouth. "I feel like we're supposed to go somewhere for a long period of time. Like a few months. Not book a tour—just go, and be available, and meet people for coffee and see what God opens up."

She nodded.

One of us said, "British Columbia?"

And the other said "Yes."

And in that indescribable way that happens, we knew we'd just heard from God.

We called up our third partner, Mercy Hope, and told her what we thought we'd heard God say. And she agreed. An old acquaintance of Carolyn's mother put us in touch with Nina and she offered her home, so now we're here, the three of us.

We have a goal. We want to lead people into a deeper encounter with Jesus, and together, we want to encounter him more deeply ourselves. We are a team of three: Carolyn, who is a professional ballet dancer, myself, and Mercy, who like me is a speaker and writer. People have commented that it's almost miraculous Mercy and I don't compete with each other—that instead, we each highly value and make room for what the other brings to the table. But that's how it is. We love each other deeply and don't see in the other any kind of a threat. Likely this has something to do with our personalities (neither of us is competitive, per se). Likely it also has something to do with our sense of being companions on a journey, a couple of sometimes war-weary heroes on a quest to save the world by loving Jesus.

I know, I know. Delusions of grandeur. Or maybe truth.

Carolyn, practical, capable, and gifted at pretty much everything, is in many ways the glue that holds us together. She books our tours, schedules our calendars, and keeps us putting our feet on the ground and getting things done.

All three of us are in our thirties. We're all single. Carolyn and I have done ministry together for the last six years, and Mercy joined us three years ago. We don't have traditional jobs, assets, degrees, or anything that would mark us as successful adults in a world where success is largely measured in terms of marriage, savings, and security. But we all have a sense of calling, and we're all doing our best to walk it out faithfully.

Since I was twenty-one, I've juggled work with the other things I want to do. Travel, fiction, independent study. One key, central, like-breathing part of my life is taking time to seek God through reading and prayer. I've done this for years. Sometimes I journal. Sometimes it's an hour of Bible study. Sometimes it's just closing my eyes and listening.

Lately it's been meditative. Contemplative, to use a less-used word. Prayer that happens with an open Bible and the words of Scripture and a listening ear. I've taken to spending this time in the early hours of the morning, usually around five or six. I seek God in the shadows and listen to him speak as the sun slips up and finds its way into the grey room and starts to lighten the morning.

I'm not one who "sees" things, but last November I had an experience in that early morning time that I might call a vision. I can recall it, in detail, even now. I saw Jesus. He stood in a desert landscape like the one where I used to live. Power lines and the lights of a city marked the darkening world behind him, and behind that, desert mountains. The sun was setting.

Jesus held his hand out to me and said, *"Come past your limits."*

Now, sitting cross-legged on the floor in Nina's lower level, looking out the glass sliding door at sunlight starting to slip into the grassy strip of space between her condo and the one across from it, with a prayer book and a Bible open in front of me, I'm tired.

I'm not seeing visions. I'm struggling just to keep my eyes open.

Right now my days go like this:

Wake up at 5 a.m. Spend an hour with the Lord.

Start editing work for clients. Work five or six hours.

Go out canvassing churches. We're here for three months, so basically we're just dropping in at church offices all over BC's Lower Mainland and introducing ourselves. We do this for most of the day.

Come back and collapse. Sometimes work more hours.

Mercy and I have decided we want to write a book based on the spiritual parallels we see in the Marvel movies, because that's the kind of geeks we are. So some evenings we watch *Agent Carter* or Marvel movies from *Iron Man* forward, and we take notes and discuss ideas for the book. It's fun. But it's also work.

I need a rest.

A serious rest.

My mind is tired. Not only that, but my body's not holding up especially well. The abdominal swelling I noticed shortly after my cardiac arrest is getting worse. I feel like I'm struggling to stay focused on work and like I'm battling to keep up my energy all the time.

But meditating here on the carpet, I can sense a shift.

For many years I've understood my life as following a biblical pattern.

It began with the call of God in the California desert. The real encounter with a real God, a real Jesus, that changed everything for me. I fell passionately in love. I wanted only him.

But that kind of spring morning often gives way to a long winter, and mine did. All emotional connection to the reality of God vanished. I found myself struggling to feel any connection, any faith, any love at all, going either direction. I begged God to tell me what was happening, and he gave me Deuteronomy 8, about the journey of the Israelites in the wilderness for forty years and what God wanted to teach them there. There are things, essential things, you can only learn through adversity, hardship, and lack.

I was going into a wilderness, not because something was wrong, but because I had something to learn.

Twelve years passed.

In the air on the way here to the city of Abbotsford, British Columbia, I heard the Spirit of God say, *You're coming to the river.*

This is Abba's Ford.

The place to ford the river—into the promised land.

This is border country. A changing place. You're transitioning.

You're not in the wilderness anymore.

KNOWING SOMETHING IS NOT THE SAME THING AS DOING IT

I FEEL LIKE TRYING TO EDIT full-time for clients—a job which means completely immersing yourself in someone else's thoughts, someone else's life, someone else's mind, and interpreting and clarifying all the thoughts you think after them—while also trying to be present with God, and with my friends, on this trip … like it's going to burn me out.

Like I'm not going to be *okay,* if I keep trying.

But what else can I do?

The answer is pretty obvious. I've got thirty published books.

But marketing didn't work, I tell myself.

The correction is pretty quick in coming. Maybe because I'm honest. Maybe because the Holy Spirit is good at highlighting where I'm being a hypocrite.

You can't say it doesn't work. You didn't do it. You did two easy things and then you quit.

But I knew all the other stuff to do, so I felt—I *felt*—like I was doing it.

It comes like a flash of lighting, one of the most valuable lessons I have ever learned: *Knowing something is not the same thing as doing it.*

WHAT A WEBINAR CAN DO

HERE IN CEDAR-SHADOWED, rain-dripping Abbotsford in the springtime, we are only a few sloping streets over from Columbia Bible College, one of Canada's largest Bible schools. Some new friends invite us out to hear an author and former pastor by the name of Mark Buchanan, who will be speaking on rest. His lecture is like a message directly from heaven to me.

Mark is Canadian but every inch his Scottish ancestry: he's a broad-shouldered, balding poet; someone you'd expect to carry a broadsword and a harp. He speaks of our culture as "Pharaonic." All work, all driving forward, all our identity wrapped up in what we do. Pharaoh cut off the Israelites' supply of straw and mud to make bricks and then ordered them to double their daily output.

I realize my work, or at least the way I approach it, has become Pharaonic. Energy, health, passion, and desire to do it are all dwindling, but the demands on my output are greater and greater, and I can't do it anymore. I realize, like lightning, that to be faithful to what I believe God is asking of me—the travel, the ministry, even the writing—I can't keep trading my hours for dollars. It's not sustainable; *I* am not sustainable under this model.

What would be sustainable, and smart, would be to build a business based on passive income products. Like books.

Mark is inspiring to me because he himself is an author, a teacher, a speaker; because he's being paid to come here to Columbia and speak; because he left his pastoring job some time ago to focus on exactly the type of work I want to do. To speak, to write, to message the truth he sees.

That is what I want to do. Need to do.

I go back to Nina's lower-level apartment determined to change things. I crunch some numbers and realize I can give myself the rest of our trip dates off if I want to (sometimes I am the only Pharaoh cracking a whip over myself). My finances will manage, and none of my deadlines are urgent or even expected quickly.

I'll use my newly freed-up time to (1) be more fully present on this trip and (2) build a business around my books.

I finish the few details I can't push off and then stride forward toward my new career.

Step 1: Implement more pieces from 10k Readers, the ones that take more than thirty seconds to do.

Step 2: Watch a webinar.

A while back I got on the email list of a guy named Tim Grahl. Tim is a book marketing expert, a quiet and self-effacing self-proclaimed introvert who, as far as I can tell, sits at home on his computer and helps authors hit #1 on the New York Times bestseller list. Probably he can tell me some helpful things.

He happens to send me an email about a webinar he is cohosting. The guest speaker is Jeff Goins, another author. The name of the webinar is "How I Built an Audience of 100,000

People in 18 Months."

Both of these guys are smart. They're not sleazy, and they're not selling snake oil. Their message boils down to a few key things:

> **1.** You need to figure out your message.
>
> **2.** You need to work hard to build an audience. If you have an audience ready and waiting for your work, you will no longer have trouble

"marketing" your work. But if you work hard at this without a good system, you'll waste a lot of time and effort and keep spinning your wheels. So …

3. You need a good system.

They lay out such a system. It's simple, it makes sense, and it's very much what I learned from Nick Stephenson a few months ago and never followed through on.

I begin to take action on what they teach immediately, and as part of that, I decide I will spend money on building this business. I'll treat it like a real thing, a real business. I'll treat myself like a real author. For years I've done this "hobby business" thing, as though I think I can become successful by accident.

That doesn't happen. No Olympic athlete, when he stands on the podium and receives a gold medal, tells the media, "You know, I didn't think I was going to make it. I gave up halfway through the race and figured, 'Eh, whatever, I'll just coast from here on out. I'm as shocked as anybody that I'm up here."

If you work hard and persistently, with good systems and models in place to give you leverage and expedite your results, it doesn't guarantee you'll succeed. But if you don't *intend* to succeed, you won't.

At this point my head is beginning to spin with the possibilities, and I feel like God has opened up a reservoir of knowledge for me to drink from. It happens to be "launch season" for a lot of big-name teachers in the online marketing space, which means that—following the "value-first content marketing" model, which I will come to understand in much greater depth as I go—they are teaching webinars, doing three-video workshops, and handing out blueprints and how-to PDFs for free.

Once you get onto the email list of one of these guys, it's a bit like falling into a pool. You weren't wet a minute ago but now you're soaked. Jeff Goins emails about a guy named Eben Pagan, who is not really an author—he's an online business "guru," somebody who teaches about online business on a much, much bigger scale.

Eben is launching a $10,000 program called The Virtual CEO, which even if I could afford it is beyond my current scope in terms of what I actually want to do. But Eben, more than any of these other guys, lays out a compelling vision for what an online business can be. He explains how the world is changing and why now is the best time in history to be a teacher, an entertainer, or anyone who can provide creative or instructive content online.

I watch his three-video series, and things really and truly change for me. Now it's not just about trying to sell some books so I can make some money and spend less time editing, and be less stressed out when I'm on the road with my team and get more time for sleep and exercise. Now it's about changing the world. I realize as I watch that I can devote my life to communicating the messages that are most important, and not only will growing my business pay my bills, it will reach people in a way that matters.

One thing Eben says really sticks with me. He says (paraphrasing), "We need to stop thinking about how we can make money, and instead think about how we can create value. As we bring value into the world and positively impact others, money and growth will follow."

It sounds to me a lot like "Seek first the kingdom of God, and all these things will be added to you."

I can do this, I realize.

I can write, but I can do more than that. I can use my writing and *even my marketing* to make a real change in my generation. To teach, to minister, to unfold the gospel in powerful ways.

And I can make a living while I'm at it. One that isn't Pharaonic. One that doesn't require me to make bricks without straw, or trade all of my time for money, when time is so infinitely more precious and more valuable than money could ever be.

CONVERTKIT

THE FIRST THING I DO, the first investment I make in my new business (besides the earlier investments in training), is to sign up for a paid email management service called ConvertKit.

ConvertKit is a beautifully designed, intuitive, and easy-to-use way to gather and talk to an audience. I sit up and pay attention when Tim Grahl recommends it in his webinar because in the past, he always used and recommended MailChimp. ConvertKit starts at $29 a month and goes up as you add subscribers. I could continue using MailChimp's free service, but I switch over—knowing that I'm drawing a line in the sand by doing so.

That $29 a month (more like $32 for me, in Canadian funds) is a statement to myself that I am taking this thing seriously. That I am truly going to do it. That I'm not just a hobbyist anymore.

If I was holding back before, I'm not now.

I'm in. I'm in all the way. I'm going to do this thing until it works.

YOU HAVE TWO JOBS

YOU HAVE TWO JOBS, Eben Pagan said in his video series: *making and marketing.*

Actually, what he said was something more like this: There are only three activities in your business that make money, and you must focus on doing those things. Those three things are product creation, marketing, and customer service.

Since at this time I have no customers, I latch on to the first two.

Making, I am already pretty good at.

Marketing, here we come.

MARKETING (SLOWLY)

"MARKETING," IN THE ONLINE WORLD, means essentially three things:

1. Reaching an audience with valuable content (usually free).

2. Getting permission to stay in touch with that audience (ideally by having them opt in to an email list).

3. Staying in touch, and being—to borrow Tim Grahl's phrase—"relentlessly helpful."

I sometimes teach this now, and I usually use the framework "Engage, Give, Serve." But looking at it as I write this book, I realize how much I owe Tim for the general idea. Not that it's unique to him—this is what pretty much all good online marketers, in all niches, teach.

"Marketing" in the digital world is not the buy-my-book-flogging, elevator-speech-giving, stand-on-a-podium-and-shout kind of business it always seemed to be. It's not fundamentally a matter of cocktail party networking, doing deals, or running ads. It's about showing up with valuable content, helping people, offering something of worth, and inviting them (sometimes) to get more value by buying something from you.

You can write a sales email that is valuable to your readers even if they don't buy anything, and a thousand times more valuable if they do.

Marketing can be missions; it can be ministry.

Knowing *that* changes everything for me.

Following the framework above, I do three things:

> **1.** Finally figure out that I write for Christians, and my core message is the kingdom of God and developing a healthy, vibrant, and Bible-based spirituality. For a lot of years (while I was a "hobby publisher") I tried to sit on a fence regarding my audience. *My books are Christian ... but they're kinda crossover ... and honestly I'm a little concerned about getting theological hate mail ... and I* would *like to reach non-Christians with the message of Jesus ... and*

how big is the Christian fantasy market anyway? Might be shooting myself in the foot to focus there. After doing this for a long time I finally figured out that my ideal audience is people like me: Christians who like fantasy-type fiction that speaks into their spiritual lives and sparks growth and deeper understanding. Clarity on that would allow me to target my marketing effectively, rather than doing the kind of "fire a cannon out of a canoe" messaging I was doing previously. Knowing my audience is bedrock, and it finally gives me freedom to move forward.

2. Decide to give away my books *Exile* and *Worlds Unseen* (both first in series) for free, in their entirety, in exchange for an opt-in. In the world of online marketing these are usually called incentives. I like to think of them as gifts with an invitation attached.

3. Set up my email lists in ConvertKit so that people will automatically receive their incentives when they opt in to my email list. And then set up an autoresponder sequence advertising all of my books, while crafting each email in the sequence into a message that I feel matters, and which I hope will be edifying and minister to people on my list. Whether they buy books or they don't. I write all of these emails on my phone, while riding the ferry back to the mainland from Vancouver Island. The weather outside is too cold, rainy, and foggy and dark to see much of anything off the side of the boat, so I stay indoors and thumb-type. I enjoy writing them, and I feel so much hope.

With all of these pieces in place, there is nothing left to do but find ways to reach new readers. Nick Stephenson lays out a lot of these in his course, so I start to go through the list.

1. Giveaways. I give away books in my genre, and Kindles. I have a few hundred people on my list and ask them to tell their friends, and hey! List growth.

2. "Reader magnets." This is a Nick Stephenson term (he has a book by the same title. I think it's free—because it's a reader magnet—so if you want to learn to do this, I'd recommend you download it). Basically, a reader magnet is a book you give away for free on Amazon. This allows you to reach readers in your target niche or market. You include an opt-in at the front and back so that people get on your email list in exchange for more free books or other content.

3. Keywords and categories on Amazon. This bit is important to make reader magnets work, because putting your book in the right keywords and categories means your book can actually be found. Amazon's slush pile is very, very, very, very deep. It is a slush abyss. You don't want your books to sit at the bottom, and I know this because most of mine have. I tweak this on Nick's advice and try to follow his instructions, but in actual fact I have no idea what I'm doing and I cut a lot of corners. It still does help, if only a little bit.

4. With all of the above in place, I start running regular promotions for my free books through "book promotion websites," a special species of promotional machine exemplified by BookBub and including names like Book Gorilla and Freebooksy. These companies build up massive lists of readers who have expressed interest in particular genres. You pay to have your book featured in an email to those readers, only when your book is free or for sale. With that kind of targeted traffic going to my reader magnets, I start being able to add to my list in small numbers and also watch my income go up per month—by $50, $75, $100.

Growth is not astronomical through doing any of these things. *But it does happen.*

In the spring, when I get started, I have 289 people on my email list. Most of these have been scraped together over many years, and they aren't really my target market. (A lot of them joined my list when I ran a contest for young homeschoolers, years ago. So it's homeschool parents for the most part.)

By the summer, I've built the list to about 2500 people and moved up to ConvertKit's next pricing tier. That's fine with me.

Because this is really happening.

FAT COWS AND LEAN COWS

GOD DOES NOT USUALLY SCARE ME, but once in a while ...

It's August 2016. I've been working at "becoming a full-time author," "building my list," "marketing my books"—whatever I happen to be calling it at the moment; it fluctuates with my own sense of grandeur and motivation—since the end of March.

Let me be entirely honest.

Sometimes I am really excited about this. I remember how I felt in BC. The urgency for a change. The sense of crossing over—out of the wilderness, into the border country en route to the promised land. The call to rest. I remember the flash of vision, of understanding marketing-as-mission.

At other times, editing is cushy, familiar, and lucrative,

and list-building / authoring feels slow and foreign.

The time off back in the spring helped me reset, physically and mentally, and I don't feel nearly so desperate now to escape the time-for-money career model.

(Let me also be clear: That model is a fine one if God is calling you into it. I have no problem with anyone taking a path other than mine.)

Anyway, sometimes my motivation wanes.

On this day in August, I am hiking around a tiny lake.

I found it—by accident—because I took an overgrown path through the trees on the other side of a sketchy-looking gate in a fence.

You push down a shady path that winds through weeds and tight-in trees, where you feel like you're going to be strangled by the undergrowth or eaten alive by mosquitos, if the poison ivy doesn't get you first. The kind of path where you pull your arms close to your body and huddle as you walk because the trees are all reaching for you and the plants along the way are brushing against your legs with wet, muddy fingers.

But then you come out all of a sudden where there's light. The path widens, opens up, and splits in two directions around a small lake. Mud Lake, the sign on the fence said. It's far, far prettier than the name indicates.

Maple trees and oaks and quintessentially eastern Canadian hardwoods whose names I don't know grow around the perimeter. Some of their leaves are already starting to turn yellow, red, or orange, and they reflect off still water in the lake. Ducks preen themselves in the water just off the bank, and shiny-shelled turtles sun themselves on logs and rocks. One twisted, bent tree arcs out over the water from an open patch of bank, where pines have dropped a carpet of rust-colored needles.

Walking around the lake takes you through natural arbors where the sun filters through young trees bent over the path, over a boardwalk bridge across the water where ducks seem to float and dive at eye-level with you. It takes you across grassy lawns and through mysterious fairy woods, the air hushed with pines and slanting light, the way marked with fallen logs.

It's like stepping out of the city and back into childhood, delight and discovery around every bend. I have to get back by a certain time because I'm responsible to teach a class in the afternoon, so I take the path around the lake with a certain racing of my heart, just hoping I'm timing it right and this path won't turn out to be one that takes hours to traverse. I only intended to take a short stroll this morning but now I'm hoping I can just go and go, ten or twenty kilometres, and come back sweaty, muddy, and exhilarated just in time for a shower and teaching.

While I hike I pray, and an image strikes me with terrifying force.

The image comes from Genesis, the story of Joseph. Pharaoh had a dream: in it he saw seven fat cows and seven fat ears of corn. But in his dream there came up seven wasted, blighted, and lean cows, and seven lean ears of corn. The lean cows and the lean corn devoured the fat cows and the fat corn, yet they remained wasted themselves and did not grow any fatter for their violent and cannibalistic feast.

What I see in this is that I mustn't give up on the path I've set upon in business. Client work, with its relentless trade-off of time for money, is for me a lean cow, a lean ear of corn. It will devour the fat cow—the work, the business model, the commitment to writing and communicating—that would have brought abundance, *and the lean cow will not grow any stronger for it.*

Somewhat to my disappointment, the path around the lake doesn't take more than an hour to walk, and my anticipation of pushing both my body and my deadline as far as possible doesn't pan out. But I go back to my friend's house with my mind buzzing. I feel a sense of fear, the good kind of fear that sobers you and keeps you on the straight and narrow. I know that flash of insight came from the Lord, and with it a mandate and a renewed sense of urgency.

I do not yet understand fully why it's so important that I make this change—why it matters so much that I don't slack off on my commitment to replace client work with passive income. Only that it is, that it does. In this matter I've had vision, I've had inspiration, I've had ideas. Now I also have the fear of the Lord.

FATHERS LET THEIR KIDS DO CRAZY THINGS

THAT SUMMER I TRY out something new. It's the next logical step in Nick's program, but it's a lot more technically challenging, and it also involves spending—potentially a lot—of money.

I'm going to try paid advertising.

I've done the book promotion sites, but this is a whole other level. The advertising platform is Facebook, with its worldwide reach to over a billion people and its frighteningly detailed amount of demographic information.

(Yes, I do have conflicted feelings about online privacy and advertising. But to be perfectly honest, I'm mostly in favor of advertising that's personally targeted, both as an advertiser and as a consumer. It means not only can I directly reach out to people for whom my work is relevant, but I also personally get served a lot fewer irrelevant and offensive ads, and a lot more I'm really interested in.

To me this is part of the power of the Internet to connect us. And connection makes powerful things possible. Yes, we need to be aware and responsible. But it's far from being all bad.)

Before I venture into this world I drop another $997 on another course: *Ads for Authors* by Mark Dawson. At the time titled *Facebook Ads for Authors,* it's a step-by-step, *highly* detailed look at how to run Facebook ads in order to build your email list and sell books. So detailed that, to be honest, I only watch two modules. At that point I dive in with the knowledge I have and start figuring things out, and I don't come back to finish the course. Will do, one day.

I start advertising on Facebook using a photo of two rowboats from Unsplash.com (my favorite source for graphics) and wording that directly targets fans of authors whose genre is similar to mine. The book I'm advertising is *Exile*. It's free. I'm not asking anyone to buy with these ads; I'm asking them to receive a gift, an entire novel. They get on my email list in the process, and if they like what they read—both in the book and in my emails—they'll stay.

It's building an audience, and in the process, something of a community.

Results are immediate.

For perspective, in May I added 16 subscribers to my email list. In June I added 3.

In July, with my first ads running at a fairly moderate budget, I added 640.

At first, of course, that just means a lot of money spent and a nice graph in my ConvertKit account. But my previously written autosequence is set to actually advertise another title three weeks after a person joins.

Three weeks after that first run, I watch as the graph on my Amazon sales chart starts to creep up. I quickly run some numbers and realize I've tripled my advertising dollars. Amazon doesn't pay for sixty days past the end of the month in which the sale occurred, so it's roughly a three-month wait for the payout ... but on paper, at least, it's there.

In August I spend more money, and I start running a similar ad for *Worlds Unseen*. Again, it's a free book. I'm not selling anything. I'm offering a gift.

Results: 1094 new people opting in for *Exile*; 555 for *Worlds Unseen*. And people are apparently also visiting my Amazon listings in new numbers, because opt-ins on my reader magnets are suddenly in the hundreds as well.

And ... for the first time ever, my paperbacks are starting to sell. I don't advertise my paperbacks.

Three weeks after I up my ad spend, my sales go up again. Higher than they've ever been. I've tripled my money again.

In a breathless moment at the beginning of September while I'm visiting my parents in my old hometown, with the memory of fat cows and lean cows still burned in my heart, I realize that if I scale up faster than I intended to do, I might become a full-time author overnight.

(Well ... sans that three-month wait for a payout.)

It means putting a lot of money on credit cards, and while I have the room, and sales are performing so far, I'm not sure about the wisdom of it. I am, at the same time, buying a house with Carolyn. And a new used car, as my old one is on death's door. It's more financial responsibility than I've ever, ever had—but I've also never, ever seen performance like what's happening to my books because of my ads, and I've never dreamed I could build an audience this big and this engaged so quickly.

It strikes me, in a way that makes me cry a little with the revelation, that all I'm doing is finally putting a match to the fuse of years and years of labor and investment. Most people, when they want to become authors, don't enter the field with over thirty titles already written and published. Most haven't already spent decades honing their craft and trying to be faithful without seeing any return.

The enormity of possibility is overwhelming, and I go for a walk by the river to clear my head.

On the way out the door I tell the Lord, "I just need to hear from you about this. I want to do it, I think. I just need to know it's okay with you. I know it's kind of crazy."

It's a beautiful day, and I walk several kilometres lost in thought and prayer. And then I look up and see something I remember, here in the city where I grew up.

Some of the parks along the water have fairly steep, grassy lawns leading down to the flat cement sidewalks that skirt the river's edge. As children we came here, my sisters and I, and those grassy slopes looked like mountain heights. We would roll down them all the way, landing in dizzy, gasping heaps.

They look smaller now, but still.

Earlier on the walk I noticed a father with two little children, one in a wagon. They seemed sweet and were clearly having fun. Now one of the children is perched at the top of the hill, in the wagon, and the father is urging him to come racing down.

I smile to myself and think, *If that was his mother, she wouldn't let him do that.*

And a thought comes back, an answer. To my observation and to my request.

Fathers let their kids do crazy things.

In the beginning of September, I start to run ads for nearly $200 a day.

SEPTEMBER

IN SEPTEMBER I ADD 6291 new people to my email list, and my sales climb proportionately. Books I couldn't get reviews for have now been reviewed over a hundred times each. (Mostly four and five stars, to my relief, pleasure, and surprise.) I'm getting email from readers every single day. Thanking me for my work. Thanking me for my emails. Telling me that my books are touching their lives, sometimes in shockingly deep ways.

This, I didn't foresee.

I knew I wanted my writing to be ministry, my marketing to be ministry, but I didn't realize until the emails started coming how much my fiction *could* actually be that, just as it is. I start to believe in my books in a very new and different way. To believe that they are more than just entertainment—that they're truly valuable: because God chooses to speak through them, and readers choose to bring their hearts and minds and invest themselves in my stories and find meaning there.

This is amazing to me, and it charges my whole self-concept for this author thing with a new and stronger sense of purpose. Suddenly my readers have names, and stories of their own which they generously share, and questions and opinions and, so very often, thanks.

When I was seventeen and writing a screenplay in the breeze off a swamp cooler I didn't know this. I didn't know that "draw out your soul to the hungry, and satisfy the afflicted soul" didn't have to mean feeding someone bread and vegetables. It could mean feeding them words, stories, perspectives. Truth, I hope.

To know it now is humbling and amazing to me.

On a very personal note, I almost can't put into words what it means to hear from people every day about stories I used to have shoved in a drawer or under my bed, manuscripts I poured myself into and never really thought anyone would read. I had tried to find traditional publishers for my work but eventually just gave up, and the move to indie publishing—much as it suited me far better than the traditional model ever did—didn't fix the fundamental problem that I didn't have readers.

But now I do.

It means a lot.

This is an enormously eventful month. Not only because of the business, but because Carolyn and I find and buy our house. It's enormous. Forty-six hundred square feet in a small town called Crystal Beach; two open-concept floors. Four bedrooms and two full bathrooms. Not at all the tiny cottage with a double-car garage we were looking for. The thing is, our one sticking point for a home was that Carolyn needed space for a dance studio, and in this place, all we had to do was roll our vinyl studio flooring out where a normal person's living room would be, and we were set.

As well, my friend and fellow author and editor Susanne (C.S.) Lakin bought me a plane ticket west to join her at a writer's retreat in Lake Tahoe, which she's hosting. I agreed to help teach. I fly out three days after Carolyn and I move into our house, while I'm still sore from the elbow grease of our first deep clean (4600 square feet, let me remind you). Thank God for church friends and family, who came and helped and hauled and cleaned.

In Tahoe, about ten people meet in a beautiful house on the mountainside. You can just see the lake from the upstairs windows. Everything here is Western: the air, the light, the Ponderosa pines. It wakes the traveler in me, and the girl who lived in the desert and found God there. Susanne cooks gourmet breakfasts for all and keeps coffee and wine on hand. She and I have never actually met before but are instant friends and a little eerily alike. We love to write, drink coffee, and hike; and we do all three, in between teaching sessions.

I teach and critique as an editor, but I do it keenly aware that that's changing. That this may never be my job description again. The whole time I'm here I'm getting upwards of ninety emails from readers every day, and I feel like it's a full-time job answering them. Around nine o'clock at night as I sit with my old, dying laptop at the ornate dining room table, one of the other writers says, "Are you still answering fan mail? I hate you!"

At the end of the week Susanne and I throw ourselves off the top of a mountain on a zip line, 6500 feet down toward the lake.

Retreat over, everyone else goes home. I check myself into the local Holiday Inn for one more night before I'll shuttle back to the airport in Reno and fly home. I wash my hiking boots in the bathtub, pull on sneakers, and walk down by the lake, where I end the evening on the patio of a little Greek restaurant drinking cappuccino and listening to a gifted young couple whose music drew me in despite myself.

In the morning the light on my phone flashes to say I have a text. It's my sister Becky. It says, "Happy resurrection day."

It's September 19. I'd forgotten the date.

Two years ago I was dead, for twelve minutes.

And now so much—everything, really—has changed.

BALANCE MAY VERY WELL BE A MYTH

I FIND MYSELF, at this juncture, facing more freedom than I've ever had and also more overwhelm. On the one hand, I am rapidly growing my income and my reach just by running ads, which need, what, a few minutes of attention per day? Per week? Mark Dawson, from whom I learned to run ads, starts every day by downloading data from all of his sales and ads channels, putting it all into a spreadsheet, and studying them.

That's why Mark teaches a course on this stuff, and I do not.

I am thrilled to being making real money from my books. But there's a strange feeling of helplessness also, when your future is dependent on performance which you can only measure after the fact, in graphs that tell you where you are, and which you can't control. My ads haven't scaled as well as I wanted them to, and I definitely no longer make three times what I spend, but I'm not sure yet how to measure what I *do* make and how to calculate what I can afford in the future.

Simultaneously, I'm a new homeowner with a new plethora of bills, down payments (it turns out everyone wants a down payment when you buy a house, on everything from electricity to the Internet), necessary immediate renovations, potential renovations to think about for later, chores, and other demands on my time. And I'm still receiving upwards of 100 emails a day.

I also have books I want to write and other creative projects I'm excited to explore, like audiobooks and a new website. And I have an audience waiting for them.

Oh, and did I mention I still have editing clients? Plenty of them. With manuscripts and deadlines. My heart and mind have already moved into my next career; I'm not an editor anymore in my soul. But I do need to make good on my commitments and take care of my clients, who for so long have taken good care of me.

I'm beginning to see that overwhelm could be a problem.

The swimming pool of online business experts has continued to get deeper for me, and among those I'm now following is Michael Hyatt. The former CEO of Thomas Nelson and now head honcho of a company I can only describe as built on creative communication—a concept

I find exciting and inspiring—Michael too has a course for sale, and although I'm rapidly running out of money or room on credit cards (sixty- to ninety-day payouts, remember—I won't see the fruit of all of this spending until the end of November), I buy it. It runs me about $497 and it promises to help me get free.

It's called *Free to Focus*. It's a course on productivity. Michael's tagline is "Helping overwhelmed high achievers," and although I wouldn't have said so in the past, right now that's me.

Free to Focus lays out some very powerful principles and frameworks, which I grasp at as at a lifeline. Michael's core idea is that it's possible to become more productive by working *less*. Step one of doing that is figuring out where you are uniquely gifted: where you excel, what you do that matters. And then of course, figuring out what actually moves the needle in your business.

It takes me back to Eben's "your job is two things." Making and marketing.

And as much as I possibly can, I want to meld those two things together, so that my marketing is making and my making (almost) markets itself.

Everything else you have to do, that isn't in your wheelhouse, that doesn't fall within your unique ability and what Michael calls your "Desire Zone," really should be automated, eliminated, or delegated. This goes against my grain, because I feel as though all things should be within my responsibility and capability to do, but I can see the sense in it. The reality is, as Greg McKeown points out in his excellent book *Essentialism,* everything in life is a trade-off. To do one thing is to choose not to do something else.

It's all too easy to prioritize lean cows over fat ones, until you have nothing left.

What is hardest for me right now is realizing I can't continue to answer my own email.

I take time to work this issue through. I walk to the warm shore of Lake Erie, just twenty minutes from my new house, and sit on the beach and pray. I run pros and cons through my mind. These are real people on the other end of my inbox, my readers, and I care about them. They honor me by writing, sharing their lives, sharing their thoughts. I've been writing every last one of them back, and sometimes getting into correspondence, but I finally come to terms with it: I can write to hundreds of people, one at a time, and make some impact. Or I can write books and stories and articles that can reach hundreds and thousands of people *each.*

I honestly can't do both.

Although my finances are still uncertain at this point and

I'm concerned about keeping up a sustainable income going forward, I decide to hire an assistant. Mostly I need help with email, but I can probably find other tasks to delegate as well. Like it or not, what I'm doing now, as an author, is a business, and it's too big for me to handle on my own.

I take a Michael Hyatt recommendation and apply for a virtual executive assistant through a company called Belay. They are not the cheapest route, but I know they'll match me well and save me time on trial and error. I think it was a good decision. When they find me a "fit," they send her resume over and I almost cry. Theology student, background in ministry, works for another Christian writer/speaker, books travel, writes, does graphic design. She's also laid-back and values flexibility as much as I do … a good thing, because I can just about guarantee I would drive a more straight-laced individual crazy. She couldn't be better suited for what I need, and she decides I'm a good fit for her too. So a few weeks after starting the process of looking, I hire Monique Jennings.

While I have no qualms at all about what Monique does for me, I do still sometimes wrestle with feelings of guilt and wondering if I did the right thing over not personally answering all my email. But when I think about going back to it myself, the anxiety that grips me lets me know I made the right choice. I'm an introvert, which means not just that I need to be alone but also that I need a certain amount of mental space and freedom in order to do my work. Even answering my few non-writing related emails every week can mitigate against that.

A few weeks after Monique starts I peek into the inbox and find her telling readers who share personal struggles that she's praying for them, before she passes the messages on to me.

I did the right thing.

I'm glad.

WIDE OPEN SPACES AND LITTLE SURPRISE ROOMS

AFTER TAHOE, urgent renovations, and more housecleaning, Carolyn and I settle down enough to dedicate our house. We invite family and church family, our community, to come and pray with us. We intend to dedicate our home to God. We invite our community to bless it and us.

In our congregation, WellSpring Community Church, an unusually high level of listening takes place during prayer. It's something we all practice together, on Wednesday nights and Sunday mornings, and so when we come together to pray, you know it won't just be people who speak. It's rare for us to come together with fully fleshed-out, preconceived ideas of what we'll pray, although we do tend to choose themes. Instead, everyone listens and then shares what they hear, what they see, what Scriptures or words or images are laid on their hearts. God always speaks, and it's powerful.

In dedicating our house, we are knowingly inviting this kind of prayer. We want to offer ourselves and to bless our home, yes, but we also want to know what our Father in heaven ("Father-always-near-us," as Dallas Willard interprets that phrase—"heaven" being the spiritual realm and housed in the air we breathe, not some distant country beyond the clouds) has to say.

Carolyn and her sister Christa have made all kinds of complicated little finger foods that took approximately two days to cook and compile. If it had been up to me, I would have bought a bag of chips and some salsa … Carolyn is definitely the better hostess, and even if I sometimes begrudge what I see as unnecessary fuss and bother, in the end I can see how well she serves our friends and family—how she loves on them by paying attention to details. It's an area where I could definitely stand to grow. With everything I have on the go, and with all that I want to learn about my new business and how to run it and grow it and think about it, I feel like pulling my head out of the clouds and into the kitchen is a nearly impossible order.

People start to arrive, and I give grand tours. We don't exactly have seats. We have a lot of kitchen chairs, a deacon's bench, the ledge in front of the fireplace, a built-in window seat-like thing, and a couple of couches downstairs that were given to us by some church friends. The hodgepodge will have to do. After eating we sing together and start to pray, and then the lack of seats doesn't matter so much, because another curious characteristic of our faith community is how many people are "pacers"—most comfortable praying and walking at the same time.

Prayer quickly flows into prophecy, which is simply a way of saying that as God's people listen and hear, they speak out.

Our friend Lynne presents us with a homemade plaque, a handwritten verse tucked inside a picture frame with some sprigs of flowers and ornamental grass. The verse is one that has long been significant to me:

> "He brought me forth also into a large place; he delivered me, because he delighted in me." (Psalm 18:19, KJV)

In our gigantic, open barn of a house, the "large place" is both literal and spiritual. We know we've been brought here for God's purposes, and also that he delights in us and in providing this place for us. As laughter, singing, and conversation fill the house, that feels more tangible, more real—the smile of God in our midst.

Our friend Jim says, "The Lord is going to release tremendous creativity in this place. The writing that will come out of this place. You're going to see abundance."

And our pastor, Marc, waits until most others are finished and tells us, "As I look around this home I see two things: I see wide open spaces and little surprise rooms. And as much as those are physical realities, they're also pictures of what's happening in the Spirit. First of all, wide open spaces—you're coming into a place of abundance. God is expanding your borders, personally and as a ministry. And then little surprise rooms—this speaks of your walk with God. As you seek him, he's going to bring you into a deeper intimacy with him. As you get to know him more and more, there will be surprises and secret places along the way."

These two things together are the crux of this new season I'm in with my business:

Abundance and intimacy. Financial overflow and spiritual deepening. Greater creativity and widened borders.

All of this I sense, I *know,* in my heart is the word of the Lord for this season. I know this is why I started down the path I did in British Columbia. That we are entering a new season where the business must support ministry, support creativity, and even support intimacy—through creating time freedom and the mental space to focus on the Lord, on his Word, on learning and growing in my walk with him.

Yet I must also be fully honest and say that I feel a tension between the two, as though they pull in different directions—finances pulling away from spirituality; business pulling away from focus on the Lord. Why is this, when the whole writing business exists as an act of obedience and is built on the promises of God?

I don't fully understand the tension. Some of it, I know, is simply a practical reality: I don't know, yet, how the business will do over a long time. I don't know if it will continue to reliably bring in funds, and anyway, I have for the time being cut off advertising until I can pay down the credit cards. I am still making sales at a good, brisk pace, but I don't know how long to expect that to last. I'm in a field now where I have no past experience, no measuring stick.

Back in British Columbia Mercy played me a song called "Pioneer," by the Jesus Movement singer/songwriter Nancy Honeytree. The lyrics resonate in a new way now.

> Uncharted wilderness
> Stretches before you
> And you thrive on going
> Where no one has gone
> You travel light
> You travel alone
> And when you'll arrive

Nobody knows
But the Father in Heaven
He is glad you can go
For those who come after you
Will need the road.

Despite the explosion of growth since September, I haven't yet declared myself a full-time writer. I'm nervous about how growth may (or may not) continue to go. Besides that, I still have piles of client work to finish—which equally adds to the tension I'm feeling.

I live in an overcrowded mind. Although I do prioritize quiet time every morning, it's hard to shut the voices off. The voices of my clients and their books. That constant nag without words of financial pressure, of knowing there will be bills somewhere down the road without a definite plan to pay them—though I have many hopes. The voices of the podcasters, marketing gurus, and business writers from whom I'm learning the technical aspects of what I now do.

I need to come into a large place, a place of abundance, and also a still place. I take all of these conflicted feelings and tensions and the too-busy tangle of my mind and give it all to Jesus, multiple times a day if I must, and thank him for his grace and that he knows the end even if I do not.

LEARNING TO LAUNCH

AT THIS POINT IN MY JOURNEY I continue to be plagued by the uncertainty of whether my business can actually continue to grow.

Ads worked—better than I dreamed—until they failed to scale up another level on the very last run, and then I pulled them all down, feeling that I'd better pay off some debt before continuing to add to it. That being done, I am only growing at a trickle now, and I don't know how long to expect sales to hold on Amazon and other platforms.

I'm fairly confident that once I start to run ads again, I'll be fine. I was tripling my money in the summer; I don't need to do nearly that well, and I can still make a living. So all I need is a way to fill in the gaps, the "meantime" before I can go back to running ads, and then I'll be able to go full-time … as is so much my heart now, now that

I've seen the worth of it and tasted the idea of freedom and rest.

But I don't know how long it will be until I can do so, and with the heaps of extra bills that surrounded moving into the house, I'm uncomfortable with my debt level. Before now I've never even carried a balance on a credit card from month to month, and now I've got multiple cards that are all pretty near full. The Amazon payouts for the next few months are good—very good—but again, I don't know how long I can count on that to continue. And business growth has necessitated adding new expenses: in web hosting, assistance, more.

It's about this time that I come across Jeff Walker.

I'm not sure how I learned about Jeff. Most likely it was another recommendation from a trusted source. The world of online business, in all its niches, is a small world. People at a certain level tend to recommend each other. So I might have learned about Jeff Walker from Jeff Goins, or Michael Hyatt, or Eben Pagan, or all of the above.

I jump on his free training (another three-video series, a format which, it turns out, Jeff pioneered) because of its premise but also because Jeff is a bit legendary. I knew his name years ago, before I'd ever even considered doing something like this. It just seems like learning from the best, when the best are putting out their stuff for free, is a good idea.

Jeff's game-changing innovation, rolled out for the first time in the nineties—which in Internet time is pretty much primordial—is something he calls the Sideways Sales Letter. It turns out that to a great degree, I have Jeff to thank for all the life-changingly helpful stuff I've learned from others so far. He basically invented the concept of taking all your best ideas, packaging them as content (videos or written content), and releasing them for free over a predetermined length of time. Once you've given enormous value, earned trust, and demonstrated your knowledge and authority in a certain field, then you can ask for a sale.

It's called a "launch," and it can work shockingly well. For Jeff it has built a business that does well over a million dollars in sales every year. Throughout his videos he shares case studies, and the numbers make my head spin: this person's first launch did $2000. This person's did $30k. This one brought in $50k on a weekend with three emails.

My credit cards are tight, and I'm still not sure how everything will come together for me in the next few months, but here at the end of November I desperately want to go full-time in my chosen path, and I know I may be looking at the springboard that will allow me to do it. All I need is a way to earn money outside of Amazon: to effectively bring new products, sales, or services to the audience I've already built.

Jeff has an easygoing, no-hype way of teaching, and he lives the kind of lifestyle I truly do want: he's active, outdoors all the time, able to break away from his business for weeks and months at a time. He lives in Colorado and during the colder months of the year takes every Friday off so he can go skiing. That kind of time and headspace are what I want most, in order to pursue what I think God is calling me to—writing, speaking, creating content—and in order to pursue God himself without so much brain fatigue, so much fog, so much noise.

I'm not, at this point in my life, necessarily aware of what's exacerbating that fog.

I know it's gotten harder to focus and that my editing has slowed down—so much so that in a career where I get paid for how much I can accomplish within set hours, I'm starting to take a significant pay cut. And I'm not really sure why.

Once a year Jeff launches his paid training program, PLF (Product Launch Formula). He does it by practicing what he preaches: he puts out an extremely high value, practical, actionable series of videos that will show you how to launch a product or service PLF-style and even how to spin an entire business out of that.

I'm inspired by it again because not only is this a great way to sell stuff, it's also a great way to teach. I can see doing exactly this to inspire people and convey life-changing truth. The product launch part is the cherry on top: the potential I see is for launching ideas, starting conversations, changing lives.

Of course, when the workshop ends Jeff makes his offer. This is the highest priced program yet: it would cost me nearly $2000 to buy PLF, and I don't have that money.

But I can get a payment plan … and I think I could swing it.

I know I desperately need something to get me over the next hump.

And so, I type in my credit card number with shaky fingers, and since I won't have time to take the course between now and the Christmas season, I start planning out a launch just based on Jeff's free teaching. I call it "The Christmas Book Party." My three videos just tell my own story.

I talk about how I became a writer. Why I care about writing, the kind of difference I want to make. I talk about my favorite books and give some recommendations. I figure my readers are buying books for their kids and grandkids, so I make up some worksheets to help them figure out what to buy. (Buying books for other people is surprisingly tricky.)

I'm right away touched and amazed by the response. I did the series as videos, shot on Carolyn's iPad. They are not good quality, as I don't have any good lighting or sound equipment. My Dell laptop is so old and slow that it literally takes me a week and a half to finish the videos, create the necessary webpages, and set up a shopping cart. Tasks that should take two hours take a full day. It's incredibly frustrating. And yet, as soon as the videos go live, I realize I've never done anything this powerful. It's making a human connection my written emails didn't. People leave detailed comments, start conversations.

It's fun, and it's inspiring, and yet again I'm blown away by the power of this model to do good in the world, to create things that can touch other people in meaningful ways.

That's always been the thing for me. For so long I didn't think there was much value in my gifts. Thought writing was just something I did because I had a knack for it, but I had no real idea it could have value—not to me but to others. I always pursued this stuff with a slightly guilty conscience because I thought maybe, really, I was just being self-indulgent and should go get a real job.

But now here are people telling me how deeply they

relate, how my story is challenging them to reexamine their own gifts. People are asking how I knew writing was a "calling." They're sharing stories of childhood rejection, of rediscovery, of the Lord's work in their lives.

And it's beautiful, really. So beautiful.

This model also gives me a way to connect personally with readers again, now that I'm (mostly) not doing my own email. It's far more buffered, since it just means reading and answering comments on a few videos for a couple of weeks, rather than unlimited correspondence at all times. But I'm glad for the opportunity to be human amidst other humans, here in this digital space.

I shoot the sales video portion in my parents' bathroom while I'm visiting my hometown for my sister Becky's wedding shower. On the second floor with a dormer window, it's the only room in the house with decent light. Mind you, the wallpaper's peeling behind me and I'm balancing with one foot on the tub, but I never pretended to be glamorous.

Becky gets married the first week of December, as my "open cart" period is ending. I realize I've forgotten an editing deadline and end up doing client work in the hotel room the night before, with my bridesmaid dress hanging up in the bathroom. I tell myself the whole time I will never do this again. I'm getting free.

When the cart closes, my Christmas party has brought in over $8000 in Canadian funds, the fruit of a single week's worth of work.

Of course, I chose to put a physical product on sale, so I have heavy fulfillment costs. Only about $3000 of that is profit. But still. I can do a digital product next time if I want to. And $3000 in a week is a whole lot more than I've ever made from client work—all while feeling like I made a difference for people.

I've found my way to fill the gaps.

On the eve of giving up, the promised land is once again in sight.

PART 3:

Giants in the Land

CRASH

IT IS AT THIS POINT that things get really hard.

After my first product launch works so well, I commit myself to going full-time as a writer in the new year. I don't have guarantees. But I have enough tools that I've been able to make work in the past, enough new skills, and enough knowledge that I am—fairly—sure I can ride the ups and downs that will invariably come. Between the royalties that are still coming in from decent sales, my ability to create and launch new products, and the fall-back of freelancing if necessary, I should be just fine.

Before I can really throw myself off a cliff, though, I need to finish up my client work.

(They say you can grow wings on the way down.)

I feel an urgency about this, more than can be explained

naturally. I have crossed a line since that November 2015 when I bought Nick Stephenson's course and dabbled in taking my writing seriously. I understand myself, now, to have a calling on my life. I understand that I need to leave Zebedee and my fishing nets in the boat and go out after Jesus, because this call, this pressure, this tug on my heart is not from me.

A lot of people have asked me how you can know when God is calling you to do something. I can point to a lot of biblical principles, and I do. Where are you gifted? Where is the fruit? What is the desire in your heart?

But at some point the answer comes down to an unsatisfying "You just know"; the same thing married people always tell you when you ask how you'll know if the one you're dating is "the one"; when you ask how *they* knew.

You just know. It's a terrible answer.

But you do.

Editing has also grown incredibly hard. I used to be lightning fast and edit with ease; right now I am conscious that it's exhausting me, that I'm slow, that it feels like hard labor. The grace is gone: that's how I might describe it. I soldier on, make stringent schedules and stick to them, count down the days until I'll be done. And I begin to turn down new requests and say, "I'm sorry, but I've gone full-time as a writer."

And then it's done. The last few pages of the last manuscript. In fact it's done early; it turns out that my client (a small publisher) had accepted a manuscript from a writer that was half-plagiarized. I catch the problem, send it back with an alert for the publisher, and blink into the middle of an afternoon in which I am suddenly free.

Free forever, as far as I can see.

Carolyn and I order pizza and wings and sit on her bed watching *Planet Earth II* that night, in celebration. The wings are excellent and the film has a really horrifying scene with snakes, six-foot long racers waiting for baby iguanas to hatch from their eggs and then chasing them down before they can reach the water. I don't mind snakes, as a whole, but yikes.

What sticks with me more about that night is the sense of freedom. Of lightness and rest. Of finally being able to clear my head and do what is in my heart.

But first, we have a trip planned.

Carolyn is taking three of her sisters to Disney World in Florida, which has been for me a mecca for the last several years. In fact I'm the one who first took Carolyn there. And they invited me to go with them. It's February in Ontario, and I would love nothing better than to escape the cold here and go south.

We're leaving the very next day. In the morning I clean out my car for the drive to the airport, pack my bags in exhaustion, slowly let myself relax the tension in my shoulders and breathe easily and realize, over and over, *You did it. You're free. You're a writer, a full-time writer. It worked.*

Our flight goes out so early in the morning from the Buffalo Airport that I got us a hotel room near the airport so we don't have to drag ourselves out of bed at 3 a.m. It's an uncomfortable night on a room cot, underneath the window where there's an icy draft, but while I lie there and just breathe out thanks, I'm overcome all of a sudden with a groundswell of joy and the presence of God.

If I were to plan a retirement party for myself, a congratulations trip, a transition from one career to the next, this would be it—a trip to Disney in Florida. I didn't make such a plan for myself. I wouldn't have; I would have catapulted straight out of one thing and into the next without taking a minute to catch my breath. Maybe because there's more of a Pharaonic streak left in me than I want to admit. And somehow the timing of this trip didn't occur to me until it was upon me: that immediately after closing the door on my editing career of fourteen or so years, I'd be going south for this time away. I won't be spending the whole time with Carolyn and co.; I've packed my Bible and my notebooks, and I fully intend to get away and be with God in many of the spots I love around the resort—the coffee bar at the Polynesian; a rocking chair on Tom Sawyer island; a jungle path in the Animal Kingdom.

We land in Orlando early in the afternoon and take the Magical Express to our resort, Port Orleans Riverside. The sun is like medicine. So are the palms, the flowers. The paths through the resort, past hammocks and gardens and pools and manors. For dinner we catch a boat up the river, and a skywriter has written in cloud just over us the name "Jesus" and a huge smiley face. We head for the Grand Floridian Resort to have dinner at Narcoossee's, a posh seafood restaurant on the water.

But when I wake up the next morning, something's wrong.

I don't want to admit it. I *really* don't want to admit it. I'm up early, just because I want to enjoy every minute in this place, every minute of resting awake. But I can't clear my head, and my stomach's in knots. My back hurts.

I take a shower and wonder why the water's so cold, when I can see it steaming like it's hot.

Thirty minutes later, in the breakfast court under a giant waterwheel, I'm journaling and praying. I can't be sick. I won't be sick. I won't accept that—won't accept sabotage when this trip means so much to me. But I realize with a kind of fever-born clarity that I am not well, *in a larger sense;* that the brain fog and the exhaustion of the past six or more months, the constantly feeling tired and overdrawn, is a symptom of a larger problem.

Part of it, I think, is that my mind and my body are not at peace with each other. Heck, they barely speak to each other. Mercy loves to tell a story about when I was still in the hospital shortly after my cardiac arrest in 2014, and I was still hooked up to a heart monitor and other equipment. I brought up a subject that was inherently stressful but insisted I wasn't feeling at all stressed about it—that I was totally at peace. I thought I was. But the protest had barely left my mouth before the heart monitor started dinging distress calls because my heart rate had shot up so high.

So here, early on this February morning in Florida where I'm trying to eat or drink something that will make my stomach feel better and I am just beginning to admit to myself that I feel awful, I promise myself that I will find shalom.

Shalom is a Hebrew word; it's usually translated "peace" but it means wholeness, health, peace, prosperity—holistic wellness, of the sort where I presume bodies and minds work in tandem instead of warring against each other and telling one another lies. I write in my journal a prayer: I need to learn *shalom*.

The waterwheel turns slowly outside and my coffee burns and twists in my stomach—I still have not quite come to terms with the notion that I'm not just overtired; I am *sick;* so I'm still trying to wake myself up with caffeine. I write a psalm in my journal and then mull over a Scripture that I've never really noticed before: 1 Corinthians 6:13, "The body is not for sexual immorality but for the Lord, and the Lord is for the body."

The first bit of the passage, about sexual purity, I'm comfortable with. I have no problem whatsoever with the concept that my body is "for the Lord."

The part that's new, and that I don't understand, is the last phrase: "... and the Lord is for the body."

This is mystery! It's new and wondrous. Sun filters through the window as it won't do at home for another two months, and although I'm finally ready to admit that I'm not well—*Lord,* I give up and confess, *I feel awful*—I'm still aware of joy. I'm glad and content to be here, and I'm glad and content to have discovered a mystery, a truth I don't understand that will nestle down deep in my heart now until finally, it puts out roots and starts to grow.

That's how the kingdom works, I've found. Over the years I've seen it again and again. A word falls like a seed. Most often I don't understand it immediately. I ask. I wait. And sometime later, through a process or just all of a sudden, understanding comes and the seed begins to germinate, to manifest, even to bear fruit. It's sometimes a matter of seconds, where I hear the answer to a question even before I finish asking it (that's kinda rude, Lord, but okay).

Other times it takes years.

Decades.

I live for the answers when they come.

The trip to Florida is not what I expect it to be. For the next three days I get progressively sicker and sicker; you don't need a detailed symptom report, trust me. I am the sickest I have ever been in all my life. When the fever breaks a little and I can drag my aching body out of bed, I go outside and sit by the pool in the warm air, and I enjoy the sun and the scent of flowers. I'm struck by how happy I actually am—how joyful I feel, even content. From observation it seems that I'm happier than many other people who are here, in the "Happiest Place on Earth," with their loved ones. I observe this like a third party; not taking credit for it, simply noticing that the promises of God are really true.

From this I learn something: Happiness is not dependent on circumstances.

And something else: Contentment means receiving whatever a day has to offer and not insisting that it offer something else. It's letting it be what it is, and not what you'd prefer it to be.

They are good things, happiness and contentment. I'm grateful for them both.

I'm well enough to fly home, but once we arrive I more or less go to bed and stay there for another week. The fever is gone but I'm depleted and exhausted. I have questions. Initially I thought maybe I had food poisoning, or the world's worst case of the flu. But I ate the same meal as four other people (with weaker stomachs) and none of them were affected; likewise, all of my roommates could catch the flu from a mile away, and we shared a hotel room for a week with no adverse effects to them.

I do wonder if I simply crashed. If the push to finish my client work, and all of the stress and effort and emotion leading up to the break, caused an enormous stress release as soon as it was over. The timing fits.

I hope that's all it was. I'm still tired, and I look forward to getting well.

FEBRUARY

THE REST OF THE MONTH is marked by two events.

First, the roof starts to leak. This is bad. We knew when we bought the house that we'd need to replace the roof within a year or two; it was in visibly poor shape—much to the consternation and disbelief of the previous owner, an elderly woman who was too short to see from the ground and, we presume, was past the age of climbing up on things to look. She told us the roof was only a few years old, but from the looks of things she got ripped off by whoever shingled it.

On top of that, the roof is black. Black shingles, the home inspector told us, absorb the sun, and so they weather particularly badly.

Given how many extra moving expenses ended up on credit cards back in the fall, I'd really hoped for a grace period. But Carolyn appeared in my bedroom doorway one morning in January looking grave and informed me that when it rained last night, she could hear water running down the inside of the wall.

It was an especially rainy January, and it looks to be the same in February. Some years it's too cold for rain. This isn't one of them.

Although I still feel unsure of the future, right now I am actually able to pull money from my income and what I have saved up for taxes to pay for the roof. Taxes, I estimate, I can raise in time to pay in June, the filing deadline for self-employed people like me. So I do it. We find a roofer who gives us an exceptionally good price (with a 10 percent "January discount"), and for a few warmer days in February we're subject to the pounding of feet and hammers on our roof until the whole thing is done.

Light grey shingles, thanks.

Shortly after, Mercy arrives for two and a half weeks of writing. We've decided that 1:11 Ministries ought to venture into the same territory where I'm having such good success. Publishing to an actual audience would allow us to both bring in income (something we've always struggled with, particularly because we're averse to pure fundraising) and accomplish our mission—again, in tandem.

This whole business model—give away good content, build an audience, sell books or digital products that spread your message even further—could not be better suited to creative Christians on a mission. In fact, I feel that it might as well have been invented for us. It might be an innovation straight from heaven, revealed to Internet marketers for the sake of the kingdom.

But we need to write something before we can start to build a business on the back of it, so we've set apart this time to try co-writing for the first time. I'm feeling lighter than I have in years, because every time we've come together in the past, I've been split multiple ways—ministering, spending time relationally, but also trying to keep a full-time client business afloat and on occasion even writing for myself. This time my whole job is to be with the girls, to be fully a part of the conversation and devote myself entirely to shaping it into a finished product.

Our first day together the whole thing takes shape. We decide to write about fear, or more precisely, overcoming it. I can't remember how we chose this topic, but it likely had to do with the *Fearless* dance production we were preparing to tour in the spring. We didn't choose the topic ahead of time, or prepare. All our lives have been such that there isn't really time to think about anything until the time to work on it is upon us.

So now it falls into place: We choose our topic. We talk about it. I type up notes as we talk, on the sleek little

MacBook I bought after my launch in December. (It was expensive, but the Dell was on death's door, and I couldn't afford to let a slow computer sabotage another round of promotional filmmaking.)

Every afternoon after a two-hour session together, I go into my room and type the notes into a finished chapter. We read it over together that evening, tweak as desired, and finish a 200-page book in two weeks. We call it *Fearless: Free in Christ in an Age of Anxiety.*

It feels like a miracle to all three of us. And we're proud of the book—really proud. I've written a lot of nonfiction over the years but I'm most excited about this one. I'm certain the principles in it can change people's lives. They've certainly changed mine.

The irony isn't lost on me that I'm stepping out on a faith journey financially; that I have promises from God and a lot of very hopeful early growth, but no circumstantial certainty. There is in all of this a very strong element of fear.

On our first day writing together we asked the question, *Why does it matter?* Why does it matter if fear controls our lives? Why does it matter that we learn to walk by faith instead—that we find courage and go on, despite our feelings, despite the lies that fear screams at us?

It matters, we decided, because of the parable of the talents.

In the parable of the talents a wealthy landowner goes on a journey and entrusts portions of his wealth to his servants, each according to their own ability. He gives one servant five "talents"—a unit of weight, probably silver—to another two, and to another one.

The first two servants invest their talents and make back double what they were originally given; when the master returns, he praises them and entrusts them with even greater wealth and responsibility. The third servant, however, buried his talent out of fear of the master and fear of losing what he'd been given. The master berates him for it and throws him out of the household.

The story can seem overly harsh and unfair until we realize that the servant wasn't given some tiny portion of the master's wealth; a single talent of silver was worth around $15 million today. The servant had been given something immeasurably valuable and squandered it out of fear.

We do the same. God has given each one of us gifts that are immeasurably valuable; even the "least talented" among us has a powerful role to play in the kingdom. When we bury our talents out of fear we rob ourselves, we rob the world, we rob God.

So it matters.

And this all matters to me. It's applicable to me, because I've come to understand that my writing is a talent in the truest sense of the word, and that for me to squander it would be a sin. I see the value of my time differently; I see the impact that it's possible to make. I *know* what God is calling me to.

So even though it's a little scary, I choose to soldier on—simultaneously nervous and elated, unsure of the future and yet basking in the relief I feel at having time to rest, to create, and to dream of what's coming next. I feel as though I'm rediscovering myself, and it's a very, very good feeling.

THE SECOND LAUNCH

TO PROMOTE *FEARLESS*, we decide to give it away. Our goal is to give away 10,000 digital copies before we switch to a paid model.

But I need to do something to make money in the meantime. By March, I'm working on another launch.

This one is bigger, and it features a digital product at a higher price. Way back when I started selling books by autosequence, I decided to offer a package deal called the Lifetime Readers Club: all of my fiction in ebook form, forever, at a discounted price. I priced it at $69.99, and by the time I'd been running ads for a couple of months, it had started to sell—not in great numbers, but steadily.

I figure I can do a Jeff Walker PLF-style launch for the LRC. For the videos leading up to the offer, I again share my story, but in more depth, and with a greater focus on the idea of discovering a calling. I highlight the aspects of my story that I think can make a difference to people in their own lives—especially that early on, I didn't see value in my own gifts. I thought serving God meant doing things unnatural to me, not doing things I loved and was good at. But parable of the talents to the rescue: it turns out our callings can be largely identified by the gifts we discover in our hands. As we use them, the sense of calling is clarified and grows stronger. In a very real way, our talents multiply and result in greater reach and authority, just as they did in the parable.

This time I spend more time on the launch. I set aside time to actually take Jeff's course, and while I'm working on the launch videos, I also discover a new voice in the business world (new to me; he's well-known in his own circles). This time the teacher is Ray Edwards, a copywriting expert. I like Ray immediately, not only because his content is excellent and exactly what I need at the moment, but also because he's an outspoken believer in Jesus with a kingdom mindset and mission. Ray is doing a launch (surprise, surprise), and so I get access to what is essentially a mini-course on copywriting, from one of the best in the world, for free.

I love the launch model. If I'm tempted to doubt its value or to feel like I'm just nagging people for money (and yes, I do feel like that sometimes—head games are head games), all I really need to do is rehearse how much incredible value I personally have gained from free launch videos and the email marketing campaigns that go with them. When I've been able to buy the related products or courses, the value to me has been even higher.

Proverbs says that wisdom, knowledge, and understanding are more valuable than silver and gold and should be pursued above all things. That validates the desire to buy knowledge; to learn from experts. Education is not an expense so much as it's an investment—provided, of course, that you'll also invest the necessary time and action to do what you now know.

As I remind myself fairly often, knowing something is not the same thing as doing it.

Thankfully I'm able to escape the cold and grey again, this time by going to Texas to stay with my sister and her new husband, Kevin. The house they share with Kevin's parents has a big porch with white rocking chairs where I can sit every morning, sip coffee, seek God, and then segue into studying PLF and Ray's copywriting workshop and working on my launch. It's a beautiful, restorative time, and I don't feel sick—praise God.

Before the day my heart stopped, I never noticed being affected by the weather. But since then, temperature and especially light have a palpable effect on me. Winter in Ontario is hard. Escaping in the early months of the year to go somewhere in the south helps me in a way I can't quite put into words—as soon as I start to soak up the sun again, I feel like I'm pulling myself back from a precipice.

Besides the launch, I'm also redoing the product. Up to this point the LRC has been a zip folder full of ebooks in multiple formats. For a high percentage of my readers, that's a nightmare. Many don't see that they're supposed to download a file. Once they have, they don't know how to open it, or they can't load their books on their chosen reader—Kindle, Kobo, etc. Besides that, it's just not a high-value interface.

I make another investment by purchasing Rainmaker, a fancy website with built-in capabilities to host courses and memberships. (I barely know what all that means yet, but I'm learning.) With a bit of adapting I can turn a course framework into a simple but attractive club interface where readers can browse all their books and choose their downloads easily.

At the same time, I'm relaunching my blog. I hire my sister to help me move my old website over to Rainmaker, and as part of the process, I decide to delete years' worth of content from my old blog, *Inklings,* where I mostly blogged about writing—with forays into homeschooling, publishing info, and other scattered topics. The blog has nine hundred posts; by the time I'm done whittling it down, roughly three hundred are left.

The change is important because I've finally decided this is how I will keep my commitment made in the hospital: to teach the Bible. I actually got started blogging my way through the Scriptures—specifically the gospel of Matthew—at the end of 2015, but at this point I want to do it seriously, and I want my website streamlined to focus on it.

I'm calling the new blog, and in some sense my whole new writing-and-content enterprise, Revelatory Creative. A new name for a new vision, a new era, that has grown out of old visions, old seasons, and the using of my talents in some way—any way, really, that I could.

People ask me about becoming a writer, going into ministry, starting whatever new venture, finding their calling, walking with God—and this is what I say: Just get started. Just do something. Most of the doors you need to walk through, you'll never even reach if you don't start walking. Most of the answers you're seeking can only be found through process. "Abraham, leave your father's house and go to a land that I will show you." The land is rarely shown to us before we leave.

The launch schedule I've chosen takes about two weeks to run from start to finish: three content-rich videos spaced a few days apart, then a sales video and an "open cart" period with a definite closing date, which lasts about five days total. I have to work this one around my admittedly odd lifestyle. The first video is filmed in the guest bedroom at my sister's house, with a Texas flag blowing out the window in the background. The second two and the sales video are filmed back at my house in Ontario, and the cart opens the same day I fly out for another mission trip to British Columbia. I watch sales start to come in from my phone in the Calgary airport on layover.

They start out slow but strong enough that I'm happy to buy my ministry team a good breakfast, steak and eggs and yogurt parfaits, believing the money for it will come in.

A few days later when the cart closes, I'm sitting on a couch in a basement, across from a fireplace, with a view of the mountains out the patio French doors. I'm sleeping here, on the couch. There's a hush over the living area, as everyone else has gone to bed. I'm watching my sales in these last few hours of the day and mulling the change in my life.

Just a year ago—less than a year ago—I made the decision to go full-time as a writer as soon as I possibly could. To stop just *knowing* things and start *doing* them; to get a breakthrough in my life the only way we ever can.

I couldn't really have imagined how quickly it would happen. Or the degree to which I would feel reborn because of it. I couldn't really have imagined the lump in my throat right now. The freedom I feel. The sense of possibility—as I look out at the moonlight over the mountains, it feels like I'm looking out over a future full of meaning and full of rest; full of walking with God as fully myself, cut loose to do what I now truly believe I am meant to do.

The cart closes at midnight. When I go to shut it down, the launch has brought in just over $12,000.

THE TAX BILL

AT THIS POINT I DO SOMETHING that in retrospect was probably foolish: I allow my desire to pay off debt to take precedence over two other needs: the need to start growing my business through ads again and the need to save up for the tax bill that is only a few months away from coming due.

I use the $12,000 from the launch to pay my regular bills and then allocate $1500 to Mercy for future cover design—I do intend to write several more books this year—$500 for Facebook ads, and use the rest to pay off all but two of my credit cards, wiping out 50 percent of my debt in one blow.

It's a good feeling—but it's shadowed by a sinking feeling. In just a few minutes I've gone from my biggest payday ever to a bank account that's empty and the knowledge that other bills are around the corner, and one of them—the tax bill—is not going to be small. I haven't done the paperwork yet, but I'll likely owe in the neighborhood of $10,000 for 2016. Yes, I have saved up some for it, but the money I took out for the roof hasn't really been replaced. With my ads no longer running and my royalty payments ebbing as a result, I'm not entirely sure how to create the necessary cash flow on time.

I square my shoulders, pray over it, and remind myself that if I can make an extra $12,000 in a month once, I can do it again. Things have truly changed. My income isn't tied to my time and therefore isn't limited in the same way it used to be.

YOUR KINGDOM CALLING

WITH CLIENT WORK BEHIND ME and my big launch finished, I'm not sure what to work on next.

There are so many possibilities. I want to write a new novel. Record audiobooks. Do something more with my nonfiction. I feel like my mind and my schedule have expanded, grown wide and open and free together. And simultaneously, I'm facing the reality that when you don't know exactly what to do with your time, you'll tend to resort to busywork. Obsessive learning (in my case). Email.

Or refreshing Facebook over and over again.

Thankfully we are on tour, which means I have relationships to tend to and ministry to mind. We're doing various live events and meeting with people; there isn't a whole lot of room for starting in on some big new project.

And yet ...

Out of all the options of what I *could* do right now, a new idea rises to the top. During my launch, so many people resonated with the things I said about calling. They chimed in with their own stories; they asked questions. I see a real need, and a real interest, for solid teaching on this topic and so I decide—I'm going to record a video course, and I'm going to teach all I know about the biblical basis and principles that underlie the concept of personal, individual calling and purpose in the kingdom of God.

I want it to find people and give them wings, in the form of permission and awareness. I want them to know how valuable their gifts are.

I'll call it Your Kingdom Calling.

I start writing and recording it right away. I use the dining table in front of the French doors, and then the kitchen table at Nina's when we shift our quarters back to her house after two weeks. I'm truly excited to share concepts from the Scriptures that I know, from experience, can set people free from shame, from false guilt, from fear, and from being stuck in identities that someone has else has made for them and tried to shove them into. I talk about the original intent in creation, identity, the arts, ministry, the kingdom of God.

In early May I fly back to Ontario and go to visit my parents, where I finish filming the sixth and seventh lessons at their dining room table. The course has been a whirlwind tour of kitchen tables all across Canada. Not exactly a high-end studio … but it does fit my usual style, and being willing to film without *all conditions being perfect* allows me to do the important work of communicating what I have to communicate.

When I finally reach Crystal Beach again I'm ready to start work on my third launch, this time for Your Kingdom Calling. This time I'm facing a few more challenges. One: pricing. I have no idea what to charge for this. I've personally paid thousands for courses in the last couple of years. But of course, they were mostly business courses—directly tied to ways of making a financial return on investment.

Does that influence pricing? *Should* that influence pricing? What's the value of a course like this—made of ephemeral digital materials and time? What's the value of my time, my expertise? Is the course worth more if it sets someone on a new career path? If it becomes the catalyst for entry into ministry? If it germinates, for someone out there, a book, a relationship, freedom? What's it worth if it sets someone free from shame?

I've also learned that pricing higher puts you in a better position with greater perceived authority. It allows you to do things like discounts and pivots. And of course, it actually pays the bills—something which, right now, is pressing. My royalties from book sales on Amazon are beginning to dwindle, and I have that tax bill coming up. I am spending money on Facebook ads for my books again, but to my disappointment—and confusion—they don't seem to be making any impact on sales. I don't know why something that worked like wildfire just a few months ago is now not working at all, but that's the case, and I've essentially lost $1000 trying. A higher-priced product, if it will sell, enables a far more stable business and could even get me back onto a growth path again. It takes essentially the same amount of effort and outreach to sell a high-priced product as it does to sell a low-priced one, but the return on the former is much healthier.

I decide I'll price high to start and go lower if necessary. I price the course at $699 and plan to sell it during the launch for $287—significantly cheaper than any course I've bought for myself.

With that decision made, it's on to creating marketing videos. This time they take the form of a workshop: I'll pick my top three "aha" principles from the course and make each one into a lesson, with a fourth lesson opening the sales video. I run some ads for the workshop on Facebook and add to my list that way. I have no idea how the response will be—

this is very different from my fiction autosequence—but I'm hopeful.

The goal is to change people's lives. Whether they do or don't buy the course at the end of it—I want people to walk away transformed and empowered. I want them to feel something of what I feel, walking out this calling of mine (just without the open question that is my financial situation at the moment).

So that's how I teach. With a mind to transformation.

The workshop does well. People engage on a deep level. They tell me—this is changing their lives, and I haven't even released the full course yet.

One girl starts a new career.
Some commit to finishing their books. Their paintings. Their songs.
One starts a ministry through her blog.
Some embrace their relationships—with husbands, with children—in a new way.
Many tell me they are breaking free from shame—for the first time.

The story I hear most often is a variation of this: "I have been caring for my elderly parents for the last thirty years, and I never knew it could be service to God. I thought I was failing him because I'm not in ministry. You have changed the way I see everything that I'm doing. Thank you."

This might be the biggest impact I've seen from anything I've done yet.

And now I need to do a sales video and sell the course.

I'm nervous about it. I'm unsure about the price point. The $287 price tag feels necessary—I'm facing the very real potential of losing my business if this doesn't work out. But I also know that Christians are not used to paying for "ministry." I read a book on how to sell, and even though some of its approach doesn't sit completely right with me, I incorporate some of its other principles into my script—bathing the whole thing with prayer every step of the way.

This time the stakes are high for me. I need to make another $12,000; even $10k would be all right. It would be enough to pay my bills this month and make up the rest of the tax bill.

I launch the sales video.

Nothing.

Not a single sale comes in response.

Twenty-four hours pass; no sales. In the last launch I did, the opening day saw around 25 percent of my totals overall.

My heart's sinking. A reader emails to express shock that I would charge so much for something I want people to benefit from—why wouldn't I make it accessible to everyone? She isn't vitriolic, just honest, but I'll admit her email hurts. I answer, trying to be as gracious and also as honest as I can—explaining that I've just poured heart and soul into the free version, which I made available to *everyone;* that I've spent significant money to reach an audience in the first place; that I pay to maintain my website and email list; that I spent many, many hours creating this course (and therefore not earning money in some other way), and that I've already discounted it. And offered payment plans, for a product which, frankly, costs less than many people spend on entertainment or meals out for a month. I understand her concern, but the truth is, *if I can't make money at this, I can't keep doing it.*

And now the very real idea that maybe I *can't* make money at this is staring me in the face. Maybe the last launch tapped out the potential in my list; maybe my ads will never work again.

Maybe, after all, I'm going to have to give up.

The first sale comes in on day three. Sales continue to trickle in, until finally, by the time the cart closes, *Your Kingdom Calling* has made just about $3000.

I'm not complaining about $3000.

But it won't pay my bills for a month, let alone cover the tax bill. And if this didn't work—what about the next thing I try?

Deep breath.

I try to think through the problems. I examine the stats. Something interesting: out of the relative handful of buyers, a high percentage came from my nonfiction readers list, including a buyer or two from the new list I just built through Facebook. Maybe, I think, the biggest problem was that I tried to sell a course of Bible teaching to a list of fiction readers. The overlap of people interested in both just wasn't high enough.

I rewatch my sales video and realize how badly I'm selling from my heels. I'm not comfortable with the price, not offering great bonuses, and not (at all) at my best.

I absolutely *have to* do something about the bills coming up.

So here's what I decide. I decide that *Your Kingdom Calling* is valuable and transformative to people, and I want to get it out to more of them. I decide that I can take one of the credit cards I cleared back in March, and I can use it to build a new list on Facebook, entirely from scratch, *just* for YKC. When I did this last, the Facebook list was small, but the percentage of people who bought from it was high. If I can build a bigger list and maintain that percentage, I'll make my ad money back and make a decent profit besides. And then I can keep doing it, finding new audiences and doing new sales, until I'm back on a good footing and the tax bill is paid off.

It's risky.
Right?

I don't feel like I have any other good choice. I could try a new product, but I can't create and launch anything fast enough. By now it's the middle of May, and my tax bill is due at the end of June. My other bills are due considerably sooner.

So I do it.

I spend over $2000. I build a list of 500 or 600 new people.

And launch.

The ad copy on Facebook says the workshop is "free for a limited time."

"And what will you do when the limited time is over?" one stranger asks. "Will you then charge for what the Lord has freely given?"

Another stranger expresses his opinion of my topic—

"Absolute balderdash."

Another declares about my promise to help you discover your individual calling: "We're called to preach the gospel. End of story. No 'individual calling' necessary."

That last one makes me angry, because it's shaming—not just to *me,* as were the first two, but to everyone else who might see it. It's shaming to everyone who's ever felt a deep yearning to know why they are here. It's shaming to everyone who's ever hoped their gifts might matter. It's shaming to the other commenters on the ad, people who are expressing excitement and hope.

Most of all, it's shaming to those who've spent thirty years doing a good work and never before realized they were serving God.

I delete it.

I am still raw, and my confidence is still shaken, from the relative failure of the last launch. These comments add to that. It's amazing to me how, when you're way out on a limb trying to do something brave and just barely hanging on, complete strangers will come and try to knock you off.

They don't know. They have no idea who I am, why I'm doing what I do, or even what the content of the workshop is like. They don't know that I feel like I'm being asked to drag out my soul and give everything I have for others, and then be told that after I've bled out, I should just starve, or lose my house, or be forced to give up. Honestly, they're probably decent people in real life who would feel terrible if they knew that was the effect of their comments on a real human being. I'm well aware that what people will say on social media doesn't necessarily reflect who they are face-to-face.

It's not personal. But it *feels* like it is.

Facebook cranks aside, the second run of the workshop goes well. Attendance is not as high as it was for the first run, but again, the response is moving, even amazing. *These truths change lives.*

And then it's open cart.

No sales.

Not one.

I maxed out a credit card and lost every penny, so now not only have I *not* made my investment back, but my safety cushion for emergencies is gone.

And the tax bill is around the corner.

WHAT DIDN'T WORK

WHAT WAS IT ABOUT LAUNCHING *Your Kingdom Calling,* both times, that didn't work as hoped?

I've given this question a lot of thought and am not sure I know the right answers, but I do have a few insights I think may be accurate.

First, I probably did price too high. Even with the discounted sale price, I think people got sticker shock. An equivalent course in the business world could have sold for (much) higher, but in this case, the price didn't fit the market, and many people just couldn't afford it.

Second—and it's taken me a *long* time to realize this—the offer itself just wasn't as strong as in my previous launches. The Lifetime Readers Club was an almost irresistible offer. Not only did readers get all of my fiction for a low price, but I also got other authors to donate their books as a bonus, and I donated some of my nonfiction as well. I also promised that members would get access to my Oneness Cycle audiobooks upon completion, also for free. All in all, readers ended up paying a fraction of what the product was actually worth. In the case of YKC, the bonuses (a couple of my free ebooks and some bonus videos) were not really compelling and lacked a clear value that would make the whole deal seem worthwhile.

Second, I definitely sold from my heels, and I think I did so for three reasons.

- First, I was uncomfortable with the idea of charging for "ministry." On a purely intellectual level I could see the fallacy in this. Paul's injunction that those who preach the gospel should live by the gospel is deeply practical: *If we can't get paid for our work, we can't keep doing it. Period.* It's ridiculous to think that lawyers should be paid, professors should be paid, dentists should be paid, but ministers and independent creators whose projects are gospel-related should get blood from a stone and do everything for free. All of the above is obvious to me, but on a gut level I still felt like a charlatan asking for money, so I soft-pedaled it.

- Second, I wasn't convinced that I had the price and bonuses right. It's hard to sell when you're not fully at peace with the product.

- Third, I'd tried to incorporate methodology from a book and teacher I didn't fully agree with. This was a mistake, and one I won't repeat. The person in question is respectable, but there was a heart mismatch between me and what I want to accomplish and the approach he was teaching. Even though I tried to adapt it heavily to fit it into my mission (and honestly, I probably *did* adapt it so far it went beyond recognition as anything of his), the fact that it was there at all threw me off balance. In future I would avoid trying to learn a new system or mindset at such a critical juncture of a process. (I read his book the day before writing the sales video—when I was already deeply mid-launch.)

A fourth mistake was statistical. I don't really consider spending money on Facebook ads to have been a wrong decision in and of itself. Facebook is a powerful tool to grow an audience, and if I'd had statistically significant data to say the course would sell to my new audience, it would have been a wise move. What I lacked was statistically significant data. I had worked out an expected percentage of sales based on the previous launch, but the list size in that launch was frankly too small to give me any real idea of what to expect. One sale out of ten people may be a fluke. Until you're working with much bigger numbers, you don't have any real statistics you can measure.

Fifth, as I'd realized initially, the first launch was likely a mismatch for my audience. I built my audience around fiction, and while some—even quite a few—do connect with me on a deeper level, not everyone does.

Derek Doepker, a self-publishing coach, likes to say that there is no failure; there is only information. I gained valuable, if painful, information from the failed launch of *Your Kingdom Calling*—about my audience, my process, and even myself.

I end the month of May in a rocky place—not just financially, but emotionally too. I'm not sure I've ever experienced failure on this level before, and definitely not when success is so badly needed.

And just ahead, bills are looming.

THE OTHER THING

THERE IS ONE MORE FACTOR in all of this that I didn't mention: that in April, while were in BC at Nina's, I got sick again.

In Florida the most striking thing about how sick I got was how fast it came on. One day I felt absolutely fine—tired, but healthy and looking forward to some R&R. The next morning I woke up with a blazing fever and stayed down for weeks.

In BC the onset was even more striking because it didn't happen while I was asleep. Mercy, Carolyn, and I made arrangements to visit and pray with the mayor of a small city in the Lower Mainland, a relationship we'd formed during our three-month stay the previous year. I felt fine that morning as we prepared to go—likely a little draggy given the rainy weather, but certainly not sick. We got to the mayor's office, sat down and chatted, then began to pray … and as we did, I could feel discomfort growing in my stomach and chills starting to set in.

I didn't say anything; I didn't want to interrupt the meeting. I felt certain there was a spiritual warfare component to this, and I was determined not to hand the enemy a victory. But by the time our meeting was over, I had to be helped out to the car. I crawled into the back seat, curled up, and shook with chills and fever for the next three days.

Looking back, I realize that I never fully recovered after Florida, and with this second attack, I felt like I lost more ground. Overall I got more tired and weak, and the cloud I felt in my head—a general inability to focus and really *think*—got worse. It seemed to be hormonal. But I didn't know why it was happening.

Where exactly is the line between "physical" and "spiritual"? What is purely a matter of illness, and what is an attack from a very real enemy?

Jesus once encountered a crippled woman in the synagogue. The language of their encounter is fascinating:

> On a Sabbath Jesus was teaching in one of the synagogues, and a woman was there who had been **crippled by a spirit** for eighteen years. She was bent over and could not straighten up at all. When

Jesus saw her, he called her forward and said to her, "Woman, you are set free from your infirmity." Then he put his hands on her, and immediately she straightened up and praised God.

Indignant because Jesus had healed on the Sabbath, the synagogue leader said to the people, "There are six days for work. So come and be healed on those days, not on the Sabbath."

The Lord answered him, "You hypocrites! Doesn't each of you on the Sabbath untie your ox or donkey from the stall and lead it out to give it water? Then should not this woman, **a daughter of Abraham, whom Satan has kept bound for eighteen long years**, be set free on the Sabbath day from what bound her?" (Luke 13:10–16, NIV)

In this case the physical infirmity is clearly the direct result of satanic attack. Despite the woman's faith (she is a "daughter of Abraham"), she's bound by Satan in her body.

Yet in another case, that of the man born blind in John 9, Jesus speaks of the reason for his blindness as being unconnected to sin or apparently to demonic activity; it is simply "so that the works of God might be displayed in him" (John 9:3, NIV).

I can ask similar questions about my financial health during this time frame. As much as I can point to a handful of factors in the failure of the YKC launch, they don't fully explain what happened. They don't explain why at the same time, the Facebook ads I ran to restart my list growth completely failed to translate into sales.

Just a tactical error somewhere?
Or an attack from an enemy?

I do know that the physical struggle I was undergoing, especially the hormonal inability to think clearly, didn't help.

There is mystery in the way we live our lives, build our businesses, walk through a visible world surrounded by the invisible.

WALKS, PART 1: OVERWHELMED HIGH ACHIEVERS

IN RESPONSE to the overwhelming pressure I am now feeling, I take a lot of walks.

It takes about fifteen minutes to walk from our giant house to the shores of Lake Erie, where there's a small park overlooking the water and a boat launch. Twenty minutes with a right turn will take you to Crystal Beach itself. So every day I walk to the water, and I think and pray. I try to find my way through the challenges I'm facing—to find a solution, to identify the right hill to climb so that I can rise above this battle.

When I'm not thinking or praying, I escape my own head by listening to podcasts. It's a way to feel that I'm spending time with smart and successful people, and it lifts my spirits and teaches me things I need to know.

One of my favorites is *This Is Your Life with Michael Hyatt*. Michael is upbeat, enthusiastic, experienced, and wise. The show deals more with mindsets and life strategies than it does with the mechanics of running a business, so I don't get lost in the weeds listening to it. The tag line for the podcast is "Helping Overwhelmed High Achievers Win at Work and Succeed at Life."

Listening to the podcast actually helps me through an identity shift: I have never thought of myself as a high achiever before. I realize, as I walk toward the water, that I am one; that anybody who has written and finished and published and launched so many things, who has built an audience of 30,000 people and essentially created $12,000 paydays out of thin air qualifies as a high achiever.

And I'm *definitely* overwhelmed.

The identity shift is important for me, because I have always thought of myself as just laid-back and kind of lazy—as extraordinarily lucky and blessed but also, maybe, cheating my way through life. Reframing my self-concept so that I understand *I am a high achiever* positions me to win this fight, to get through this challenge on top. I'm not unequipped; I'm not incapable. I'm the kind of person who can get into significant battles. But I'm also the kind of person who can come out the other side.

This may sound as though I'm putting my trust in myself

and not in God. It's not that at all. It's more a matter of understanding who God has made me to be and lining up with his vision for me, rather than agreeing with the enemy's. It's about committing to see the vision through.

WALKS, PART 2: PROSPERITY WITH A PURPOSE

I STILL DON'T KNOW what to do, so I keep walking.

Ray Edwards, the copywriting teacher, also has a podcast—cleverly named *The Ray Edwards Show*.

He does it with his son, Sean, and together they are incredibly lively, funny, and frequently irreverent—in a good way, overshadowed by a deeper reverence for God that comes through all they do. Ray and Sean believe in Jesus and are mostly trying to ram it through the heads of their fellow Christians (and others) that prosperity is, in and of itself, a good thing. In fact real prosperity is essentially shalom: the holistic state of well-being that is God's ultimate will for us.

The episode content is often tactical, but it works well for me since it centers around a communication-based business (what Ray calls a "Wisdom Enterprise"). Each one also includes a "Spiritual Foundations" portion which I enjoy immensely, in part because they use it so often to poke at sacred cows. If anyone can restore my faith in the goodness of business and the virtue of asking for money in exchange for valuable content, they can. I think.

Perhaps my favorite line from one of their podcasts is Ray's response to being accused of believing in "the health and wealth gospel": "Well, I don't believe in the poor and sick gospel."

Jesus didn't come to make us poor and sick.

What *did* he come to do?

"The thief comes to steal, kill, and destroy," Jesus said. "I have come that they might have life, and they might have it more abundantly."

Does this mean he came to make us rich and healthy? Not precisely, though I believe both those things are good, received by a soul that is in good health and not made idols by the paucity of our own hearts.

Can I believe, in the midst of my panic and my lack, that I possess abundant life, here and now—that my soul can prosper for no other reason but that God walks down the street with me in my pain?

"He who has God has nothing less," says a line in a Heath McNease song, "than he who has God and everything else."*

* The line is itself a paraphrase from C.S. Lewis in *The Weight of Glory*.

WALKS, PART 3: DECONSTRUCTING TOP PERFORMERS

MORE PRAYER, more thought, more attempts at strategizing, still no idea what to do next.

So more walks.

For a while I was eating up information like it was popcorn, listening to every possible podcast, reading every ebook, getting on every email list. I've come to realize there is simply too much noise in my head, so I've scaled it all back. Now I'm only listening to a few people and perspectives that help me. That help me think, and that give me better perspectives on my life and how I'm living it, and what is possible down the road—still possible, despite the pressures of the moment.

The third podcast to make the regular cut is *The Tim Ferriss Show*. It's distinctly different from the others. I came across Tim's work years ago, the same way most people do—by reading his bestselling business book *The 4-Hour*

Workweek: Escape the 9–5, Live Anywhere, and Join the New Rich. At the time I wasn't trying to build an online business, but I did take a lot of his principles to heart and put them to work in my editing business. Despite bad press (and the cover), Tim's focus in the book isn't on "not working." It's on increasing the value of the time you do spend working by 10x, thus 10xing your output. And your impact, if that's what you're trying to make.

I have a lot of respect for Tim, who has forged his own path in many ways and seeks to make an impact through his work. If I had to pick bloggers I particularly respect as *bloggers,* Tim—whose blog these days is his podcast, with over a million listeners—is high on that list, along with Chris Guillebeau *(The Art of Non-Conformity)* and Maria Popova *(Brain Pickings).* All because they have carved out careers for themselves by being themselves; because they're countercultural even when it comes to the already unusual culture of Internet media. They remind me that I can build my business on my own terms and if I don't like the paths available, I can pioneer a new one.

Tim's podcast is all about "deconstructing high achievers and top performers," from many fields—science, health, sports, acting, politics, business, the arts. I like *The Tim Ferris Show* in particular because his guests are not people I would probably ever encounter otherwise. They all live and learn and make their mark outside of my usual comfort zone, my usual talking points; most of them way outside of evangelical culture. I find that gets me thinking intelligently about things I otherwise wouldn't and broadens my entire view of the world. It's healthy.

(It's good for us to live in the kingdom. It's not good for us to live in a bubble. There is a difference.)

Of course, life being what it is right now, what stands out most to me in Tim's interviews is how many of his guests talk about low places in their lives, when they went bankrupt, lived in a basement, made a living doing dangerous odd jobs while they tried to pursue their art or their science or whatever. Sebastian Junger, author of *The Perfect Storm* and *Tribe* and other best-selling books, talks about how for years he wrote on the side while making a living as a logger, cutting branches off trees, forty feet up with a chainsaw. It's a reminder that nobody's path to success goes straight up. Everyone who tries to live an unusual life, to make an unusual mark, to "be the change we wish to see in the world" is going to walk a path that isn't paved, that isn't straightforward, and that occasionally looks like flat-out failure—and there's a high risk of falling out of trees.

I find this immensely comforting, and it gives me hope. It also helps me remember what matters. Right now my greatest temptation is to become 100 percent fixated on the money. Many ideas suggest themselves for how I might be able to work my way out of this fix, and I reject them all because they all take me in the wrong direction. None of them are a path I actually want to go down. It's an unfortunate side effect of having become clear on my calling and vision that anything short of that looks like selling out.

NOBODY OWES YOU A LIVING, AND IF YOU GET MAD AT YOUR CUSTOMERS NOTHING GOOD WILL HAPPEN

SEVERAL DAYS OF TAKING WALKS and no brilliant flash of inspiration has struck; I'm simply going to have to work very, very hard to get out of this financial rut where I now find myself.

The setback represented by this stings. For one thing, given that I've already stepped away from editing, I'm not sure where I can possibly find work fast enough to pay the bill in the middle of June—I've only got about two weeks to make approximately $4000. That also means I'm not able to try another sale or product launch. Technically I *could,* but I'd have no guaranteed outcome, and I'm not really willing to do another major promotion to my audience so quickly on the heels of the last one. It just doesn't feel like good form, like I would be crossing a line from serving people to using them.

I decide to offer consulting, because it can pay well at an

hourly rate and is less of a crap shoot than trying another product launch under these less-than-ideal conditions. I'll look up all my old editing clients, many of whom are publishing and could use help with their marketing, and offer limited-time sessions. I also decide that I'll just explain why I'm doing it ... I need the money for taxes.

It's a right decision (probably) but not a *good* one; my heart is still lagging back in the work I was doing before ... teaching on spiritual growth, writing fiction, trying to get started on audiobooks. I'm not a fan of phone calls, and I'm already a bit exhausted thinking about doing a lot of them. Nevertheless I get started.

I'm taking a shower and thinking about all of this, and allowing myself to feel indignant and frankly resentful ...

Of people who weren't willing to buy YKC.

Who were interested in free but couldn't see the value in investing in their own growth.

Who made nasty comments on Facebook or just sent honest, frank questions over email.

God often speaks to me in the shower.

I hear him, to the effect of—*You've got to stop that.*

I understand exactly what he means. The resentment, the indignation—it will lead nowhere good. It will result in a poisoned well, in trying to serve people with a wrong heart toward them. And it indicates I'm seeing people, and not God, as my provider.

Here's what I learn in that instant: nobody owes you a living, and if you get mad at your customers, nothing good will happen.

It's easy to lapse out of love and into idolatry. Grateful to have heard God's rebuke, I repent.

THE WORK IS THE MOST IMPORTANT THING

IN THE MIDST OF ALL THIS—the failure and the panic—an unusual opportunity crops up. It's been years since I attended a business conference. But ConvertKit, my email service provider, is hosting their first conference in Boise, Idaho, and one of the speakers is a man I find particularly bracing and inspiring in the stuff that matters: Seth Godin.

This is clearly not a good time to spend money on a conference ticket, not to mention airfare et al. But when the first few emails came in about the conference, back in April, I told the Lord that I'd like to go … that if he made a way, I would do so.

And then in May, I'm offered a free ticket.

It's still a step of faith to book a flight and a hotel—but it seems like the right thing to do. Like it's the least I can do to meet God halfway.

"You know," my friend Diana tells me over Swiss Chalet, "God led the people of Israel into the promised land, and when they reached the Jordan River, they had to cross."

Point taken—we both know this story. The priests approached the river, and the flooding was high. Nothing changed until they put a foot in. When they got wet, the water parted.

Shortly thereafter, a friend of a friend who works in publishing offers to let me stay with her, free. She's attending the conference too and I can drive in with her every day. I cancel the hotel and get money back on my credit card. One more foot in, that much water splashing out of the way.

So now it's post-failed YKC launch, mid-uncertain future, and I'm getting on a plane headed for Boise.

It's probably a stupid thing to do. Most likely I should have called up the airline and begged for my money back.

But as I settle into my uncomfortable airplane seat and hurtle along with everyone else into the air, soaring at forty thousand feet above the continent in a big metal tube, the momentum and the perspective remind me that actually, life doesn't end because you have bills you're not sure how to pay.

I close my eyes and let a lot of trouble drop away, left somewhere over Milwaukee. Travel does this to me, reliably and consistently. Maybe because when I was a little kid, my dad traveled for business, and whenever he could, he took us all with him. We would pack into the station wagon or later the minivan, more kids than we had seatbelts for, and drive. Usually south, invariably late. Because we'd always left the house many hours later than planned, we often drove through the night. My parents would spell each other off, and one of the most wonderful feelings in the world was to wake up in a new place, a new state, with the sun coming up, and ask, "Where are we?" Often with the smell of gasoline tanging the air, which held that pink early morning chill and yet was still warmer and more humid than we'd left it in Canada, and of coffee with flavor shots in a Styrofoam cup (doctored up by Dad, with excitement for Mom to taste it and express how good his particular mix of shots is), as together my parents greeted a new day.

Maybe that's why. Or maybe it's because I've lived in so many places, because being nomadic has become comfortable to me—much more comfortable, in some ways, than being settled.

Travel does this to me: it makes my problems fade out, the present come back into view, and the future seem … if not exactly bright, at the very least doable.

I arrive in Idaho and snap a picture of a prominent ad over the luggage carrousel, featuring potatoes. I intend to send this to all my friends back at home who made potato jokes every time I told them where I was going.

I feel free.

It's being here. In the west. Where the sun is stronger and the air is clearer under skies that turn a different shade of blue than they do back home. With just enough room on my credit cards for food and maybe Uber. With a conference where maybe I'll learn something, but even if not, I'll feel more like a *real business person and a real blogger* because I'm here.

From the curb, waiting to be picked up by my friend's friend—Maryanna Young of Aloha Publishing—I notice you can see foothills from here and decide I want to go hiking.

Maybe I'll do that instead of attend the conference.

If travel always lifts my burdens and makes me feel free, conferences always remind me that I'm an adult and if I want to, I can play hooky the entire time and it won't affect anybody except me.

I probably won't do that.

Probably.

Maryanna arrives in an SUV, and we weave our way through traffic for twenty minutes out of Boise to Eagle, the bedroom community where she lives. On the way I get her take on the conference, the people behind it—turns out she's known Nathan Barry, who founded ConvertKit and the Craft + Commerce conference, since he was a little kid—and the area, along with a rundown of what's important about her place in Eagle: it's a got a river flowing behind it with a riverwalk along its banks, but watch out for flooding as it's been so bad this year it's actually washed some of the trails away entirely and threatened to take people with it. And if you turn right and walk about a mile, you'll reach a little café with an outdoor patio that has the best food in the region, inspired by Boise's unusually large Basque population.

It sounds absolutely perfect.

Maryanna has work to do at the office, so after showing me her apartment (which also has a little balcony looking out over a park—really just lovely and sunny and quiet all around), she takes off and I'm on my own.

That also, in a strange way, brings me to life and sets me free. I am an introvert but need and love people; too much isolation and I get lonely and unhappy very quickly. But to be alone in a new place that I can explore, just me and the Holy Spirit of God, this I thrive on in a way I can't quite describe.

It doesn't take me long to decide that I may be broke, but I need a decent meal, and an outdoor patio by the river on a warm, sunny, western day couldn't sound much nicer.

The river is indeed overflowing its banks. It's rushing along, sandy brown and white billows, under trees and bridges. It's such a very western river, if that makes sense. I've never seen one like it back east, but if you were watching a movie about pioneers trying to ford some dangerous waterway on their way to Oregon Territory, it would look just like this one. There would be oxen and barrels and Shoshone warriors watching through the trees.

The meandering concrete path along the river, under the shade of ponderosa pines and sprawling sycamores, leads eventually to the little Spanish-style restaurant and an open gate into their patio. I let myself in and find a seat beside an artificial pond, complete with fountain, ducks, and lily pads. I've brought my journal and Bible with me, so after ordering a coffee and ginger-lime chicken satay with dipping sauce, I carry on the conversation with God that started on the plane, and carried into the apartment, and then on the walk.

I'm in this surreal place internally, forced here by external circumstances: a place of hyper-clarity about my own motives. And what I see, I'm *grateful* for.

I try to walk with a pure heart always. I keep an open conversation at all times with the Holy Spirit and invite him to shine light on anything in my heart or my actions that is not in keeping with his goodness, his love, and his way of life. But for all that I am always a little afraid that I'm being directed by things I can't see, by wrong motivations; that I'm walking in self-deception.

(Honestly, I probably am, to some small degree—I'm not sure we can escape mixed motives completely in this life, or ever see more clearly than through a glass darkly.)

So all through this journey, of getting out of Egypt, of becoming a writer, of shifting away from "lean cow" client work and trying to serve an audience with books and then marketing workshops and finally Your Kingdom Calling … there's always been a little worry, in the back of my head, that maybe I'm doing this for wrong reasons. That maybe it's all about the money, or it's laziness—just not wanting to pay my dues like everybody else and work a normal job. That maybe I'm doing it out of arrogance or pride.

That's always been the fear. *But I know now that it's not true.* Because sitting here at Bardenay, knowing that I'll be spending the last few dollars of my credit while I'm on this trip just eating or getting rides into town, and also knowing that I truly don't know what to do next, how to fix the problem I'm facing, how to save my business and keep my house and pay my taxes and go on living in a good way day by day …

Facing all that, what is crystal clear to me is that the work is the most important thing.

I'm not concerned about losing my ability to write full-time because I want more money. I'm concerned because the idea, born over a year ago now, that I am not supposed to spend my life doing work for clients, that I am supposed to write and speak and make things, has morphed into a burning *conviction*. I am convinced that God himself has called me to this work, that it's important; that it's the most important thing I do. I'm convinced that people need it, even though I'm not sure what exactly "it" entails from day to day. I know I have things to share and that I have to share them.

What matters isn't that I find a way to make better money for the sake of better money; it's that I find a way to save everything so that I can keep writing my blog, so that I can write another book, so that the novel I've been kicking around for a while—entitled *Seeds*—can actually be written. It's so that I can do another course, and find ways to get the messages of *Your Kingdom Calling* and *Fearless* to more people. It's so that I can keep spreading the work I've already done. It's so that I can start building a publishing business for 1:11 Ministries as well, so Mercy and Carolyn can publish more of their own work and we can reach people with it and they can be blessed financially through it, and so all of our ministry as a team can be funded and move forward.

It's not, ultimately, about the money or about my preference for a writing lifestyle over a freelance service business, as much as I appreciate having money and really, deeply thrive on a writing lifestyle, and really, deeply feel burned out on freelancing.

It's about the work.

The work is the most important thing.

THE TAX BILL, PART 2

THE REST OF MAY AND JUNE are all about working—very, very hard.

Doing consulting calls. Doing some editing I pick up on the side. Running a small promotion or two. My friend Joe, who's been doing my accounting for several years, comes up to do the tax paperwork. Final verdict: just over $9000. I'm still short by $2k.

So I lower my head and keep going. The day I start contracting work again, I get physically ill with a sore throat and sinus problems, and the brain fog grows to epic proportions. It's a daily battle to stave off depression, get enough sleep, and try to keep my health and sanity intact. My new goal is to pay off the rest of the bill by the end of the month, only two weeks late.

Looking back, this may have been another mistake.

What I think might have been wiser would be to humble myself to the CRA and declare myself unable to pay the bill, requesting a payment plan and paying whatever penalties and interest incurred.

This would allow me to stagger payments out enough that I would still have some money to put toward growing my business again—some way, somehow.

I don't do that. I make enough to pay the rest of the bill and I pay it on June 30, and in the process I completely empty every last one of my bank accounts.

And realize, in the aftermath, that I have a mortgage payment to meet in a week. And a car payment before that. And groceries.

For the first time in my adult life, I am well and truly broke. And it feels terrible.

A MILLION GOOD IDEAS (FEAR IS A TERRIBLE DRIVER)

AFTER COMING HOME from Idaho and paying off the tax bill, I lose a month freaking out.

Truly, I don't remember most of July. I know I didn't accomplish anything much in it. I recall walking every day, running a Million Good Ideas through my mind. Trying to find the one thing to rescue my finances, the one thing that can bring in money to pay the bills—for the next day and also for the rest of the year.

I remember feeling like a walking calculator: running price points, totals and expenses, percentages, likelihoods of success through my mind.

I test out multiple possible career pivots in my mind. It isn't working just to write. I can't raise book sales enough, fast enough, without money to grow my list or advertise. My course failed. Maybe I should never have done it in the first place. So what else can I do?

I don't suffer from a dearth of possibilities. I can coach. Consult. Tutor. Edit. Critique. Do a course on another topic (maybe marketing). Start an online school. For writers. For marketers. For personal Bible study. I could write and sell content directly to my list so I don't have to wait for Amazon's payout lag. Start an ads agency and run ads for other people. Become a copywriter. Write direct sales materials for people. Write books for people. Blog for people. Ghostwrite. Start (or restart) a publishing house and publish other people's work. Find a way to get public speaking gigs. Build author websites.

I run numbers for every possibility, trying to account for opportunity costs (saying yes to one thing is saying no to something else, and possibly everything else); for the time it will take to actually turn an idea into a profitable business (I have no time); for the likelihood of doing enough sales to make any discernible dent in my financial problem (I could write and sell something to my list, but at book price points—$4.99 to at most, $25.99—and at the sales percentages I'm seeing right now, I'd probably spend several weeks to make the equivalent of a dollar an hour).

All of this is exhausting.

I have a lot of skills. Every single one is a high-value skill if I can bring it to market effectively. Yet I feel stuck, stymied at every turn, doubtful of my ability to sell anything and barricaded by the lack of a real network of business colleagues who could help me. (This is the downside of having prioritized independence, never gone to school, and shied away from business-related networking for years.)

The Internet also is loud and urgent: because I do follow several business podcasters and gurus, my Facebook feed is a beehive of ads for services, courses, and training products about how to do everything, and all of it urgent, all of it needed, and all of it promising that it can bring you millions overnight with no work required! You just have to download a freebie, buy a course or an app, learn a new skill, and apply it to an audience that may or may not be the one you already have.

All the while poverty presses down on me every morning like a ten-ton, physical weight. At times I can barely breathe.

Oh, and also—next month, the month of August, is already committed to ministry. I'm running our annual 1:11 Arts Camp for kids for a week and teaching at it daily, and then driving to Ottawa and teaching at another camp for two weeks. I'm being paid. A little bit. Other than that, I'm going to have to find a way to work and earn money while I'm away and handling the demands of teaching and camp directing.

I am, to put it bluntly, going to pieces from the stress.

I pray. And pray and pray and pray and pray.

I try to think clearly, strategize, problem solve. I have a million good ideas, but you can't do that many things no matter how good they may be, and fear is a terrible driver. Fear does not bring clarity, insight, or strength. It creates a cloud and fills it with buzzing gnats that get in your eyes and your ears.

Capping it all off … pretty much every idea I have takes me away from the vision I started out with, which has only increased in urgency. It takes me away from being a full-time Christian communicator: an author, blogger, speaker, and video-and-audio teacher who specifically explores and helps people access the kingdom of God. It takes me away from the time I need to seek God, pray, study, and walk; to live a contemplative life so I'll have something to say. I have all these ideas, *but every one leads me to owning and running a business I don't want to run.*

Despite the suffocating urgency to find a way to make money, I know instinctively this is a wrong path. The answer can't just be "build something"; it has to be "build the right thing."

I feel as though I'm at war: with myself, with my circumstances, with something spiritual too.

Where in all of this is the line between "the natural"—I made some decisions that didn't play out as I'd hoped, and that combined with an emergency roof repair and a tax bill choked out my finances; that can happen to anyone—and the "spiritual"? Where in all of this is warfare?

I know this:

>1. That I didn't choose this work; I was called to it.
>
>2. That it matters for the kingdom
>
>3. And that right now, every thought in my mind, every idea that comes to me, every bill I can't pay, is a voice screaming at me to quit.

It seems to me that the battle is a battle to hold on. That what matters most is that I *don't* give up; that I find a way to do the work that matters so much to me. The work that I get emails about, from readers or from people in my workshops or course, who tell me that what I do is making a difference. The work that entails looking into the heavenlies and then manifesting what I see, on earth as it is in heaven, through the power of words and the gift I've been given to convey them.

Amidst the chaos and cloud that is July, so bad that I don't honestly know where the month went and how it is that I started nothing substantial in all that time, I do two things to hang on to the work, because it's clear to me that I can do them and ought to. Just to draw a line in the sand. Just to say I'm not backing down. I need to say that, because *I* need to know it, and I think the enemy needs to know it too.

One is that I haul my Neo, my little writing machine, down to the water with me every day and I start work on *Seeds*. As usual I'm writing into the dark, no real sense of what I want this book to be, just a theme and some setting concepts and characters I'll discover as I write them. I commit to 1500 words a day.

The other is that I decide to fight the fear and the chaos in my head by focusing on joy every day and taking my readers with me. I start writing and sending a daily 31-day devotional to my email list, incorporating a scene from one of my novels, a Scripture, and reflections on that Scripture for each day. In the process I set up daily direct-sale links for the featured novel so I can do some sales along the way. I start writing and sending one every morning beginning in late July.

It's my way of doing the work in the face of impending doom.

Because the work is the important thing.

RETHINKING YKC

ALWAYS LINGERING in my consciousness like a wound that's still healing is the failure of *Your Kingdom Calling*. The discomfort I felt with certain elements of launching it combined with its poor reception and the sometimes outright animosity toward it have all combined to convince me the whole thing was a mistake. I can remember, foggily, why I did it—that I thought it was important, I thought it would help people, on some level I felt like it was an opportunity given by God. But I no longer really buy any of that. Somewhere in my mind I've decided it was a wrong turn and likely my motives for it were wrong too; they must have been.

But perception is a funny thing, and memories don't always tell the truth. Especially not bad memories.

I've been journaling regularly since about 2015. At the time I decided to be disciplined about hearing the voice of God, or more specifically, figuring out if I actually could and did hear from God. My strategy was pretty simple: *Write down every single thing you think God may be saying to you, via Scripture, thoughts, impressions, dreams, the words of other people, prophetic input, events or details that stick out to you.* And then just track it.

See what pans out and what doesn't. See what gets confirmed and what doesn't. Put it to the test, not as an exercise in doubt but as an exercise in learning how to discern.

It's been a life-changing exercise in many ways. There may be a parable of the talents application here too: when you invest one talent, you get back more. Make the effort to listen, pray into, and honor what you hear, and you may hear more.

In any case I hear from God a lot.

(One thing I've noticed, and it may be different for me than it is for others, but the voice of God in my life very rarely entails "marching orders" and almost always entails self-revelation—of myself or of God's self. There's a general unveiling in the direction of the future but rarely a clear-cut "do this." Instead there is a growing of relationship.)

Anyway, sometime in all the madness that is the summer of 2017, I go back and read my journal from earlier in the year, and there, to my astonishment, is an entry I'd forgotten about completely:

> *"I think this year we are supposed to call people to abdicate their fears and take authority in their own areas of dominion (see parable of the talents)."*

I did not remember writing this when Carolyn, Mercy, and I decided to write a book on getting free from fear's control. And I didn't remember writing it when I decided to use the parable of the talents as the basis for *Your Kingdom Calling,* to urge people to both discover and own their own gifts and callings and put them to work within the kingdom.

But there it is, something I felt the Holy Spirit was saying on the first day of the year and which I unconsciously carried out. Now all my questions about creating YKC—*did I miss God on this? I really thought he was saying yes!*—can rest, and while I don't understand all the aspects of this battle, I know this at least … that I did what I was supposed to do.

WALKS, PART 4:
THE GIANT ON THE SIDEWALK

SHORTLY BEFORE CAMP is to begin, I am walking down the street toward the lake and praying—over my business, my life, this town, all the difficulties I am facing. And I become aware of a giant standing in my path.

I can't explain this to you. I don't have a vision; I see nothing with my physical eyes. I just know there is a giant, a Goliath about nine feet tall, standing on the sidewalk in front of me, glowering down with arms folded.

Huh, I think. *That's there.*

I pause and linger on the sidewalk. I feel no fear, only awareness, and with it confirmation that yes, this battle is spiritual in nature. Like the taking of Canaan, this is a territory dispute; and as it was in the beginning, there are giants in the land.

I remark on this figure to the Lord before skirting around it and continuing on my way.

That evening Carolyn and I drive the thirty minutes to Wellspring for prayer meeting. At one point mid-meeting I have a strong sense that the spirit of fear needs to be called out and rebuked, so I get up, go to the mic, and rebuke it.

After the meeting a friend—who was playing bass guitar throughout the meeting as part of the worship component—rushes over to me. "Just before you went up," she tells me, "I looked up and saw a giant figure standing in the middle of the room." When I got up to the mic, she tells me, I got up in the giant's face and told it to where to go.

INSIGHTS: WHAT I DON'T LIKE, WHAT I DO

THIS MUCH I WILL SAY: I am learning more about myself through this battle than ever before.

The consultations, for example, confirm a lot of things I've always suspected. I've offered one-hour phone consultations for writers, specifically on the topic of marketing effectively. I'm grateful for everyone who signed up and really, truly care about each person and their work. I like talking to them. I'm glad to share what I can. Each and every one of them inspires me in some way.

But at the end of the day—I've thought about consulting in the past but always suspected I wouldn't like it. And it's true. I don't.

I like the people, but I don't like the physical act of being on the phone or FaceTime; I don't like spending an hour explaining something one-on-one; and I really, really don't like being tied down to specific days and times.

Having a phone appointment "on Friday, at 2:30 p.m.," feels to me like being in a chokehold.

So for all that it's lucrative, consulting isn't going to be a good plan going forward.

Do I sound spoiled? Unrealistic? Like I just need to buck up and pay my dues like everybody else? Believe me, I tell myself all of that on a regular basis. But at the same time, beneath that crust of realism is the growing conviction that all the stuff I taught in YKC is true: I did not make myself. I was designed, and my design reflects my purpose. My gifts are meant to be used. And doing things that are unnatural and life-sucking for me, that make me feel like I'm suffocating, is not a good use of *me*. It's fighting my design in a time when I am just discovering and embracing it.

Or maybe the truth is that my design is changing. That I'm stepping out of a chrysalis; that the style and form that worked a year ago will not work now, because a year ago I needed seventeen legs, and today I need wings.

I don't like consulting or appointments. What I love—and I'm really just now realizing that I love it—is making things. I realize this because in all the craziness, the thing I want to do most is the least reasonable: I want to start a podcast. I like podcasts, and I want to make one. It won't earn money. It won't get me out of this jam. I don't have the time. But that's what I want to do.

From where I sit now, the ability to do what I love—making things that are valuable, that bring revelation and life and light to others and that I can be proud of—is a long, long way away.

That's a bitter pill to swallow.

THE UNEXPECTED

CAROLYN, MERCY, AND I have been running 1:11 Arts Camp every summer since 2011. I'm the official camp director. I'm also the Bible teacher, teaching about two hours every afternoon.

This year is horrendously difficult for me.

I can't hold a thought together. I struggle to speak. I feel like I'm on the verge of a breakdown the entire week.

But the unexpected can happen in the middle of the worst times.

Since 2011, we've always opened up some of our camp evenings to a performer or two, and we've always emailed out to let 1:11 supporters know they're invited to attend. Sometimes an extra individual or two shows up, but for the most part it's just the campers and staff.

This time we are doing one of our own performances,

called *Fearless*. About an hour before we're due to begin, we notice a crowd gathering outside the lodge. We don't recognize anyone and figure it must be a group gathering to walk around the conservation area.

But then, about five minutes before we're due to start, they come in! We send staff and kids scrambling to grab extra chairs and set up whole rows because it would seem we have an audience. I go to introduce myself to a group of ladies who look vaguely familiar.

"Where are you from?" I ask them.

"Syracuse," is the answer. Gesturing to a young lady further down the row—"She's a big fan of your writing and has wanted to see you for years, so she talked us into coming along!"

Syracuse, New York?

Syracuse is *three hours away,* and located in another country.

But yes, they're here from New York. The young lady who spearheaded their coming has been following my work since 2006.

There is another group, about a dozen ladies, and I do recognize one of them as an old friend of ours from a church we attended several years back. They're talking with Carolyn and Mercy, something about a Bible study that's had a wonderful impact on their lives. *That's cool,* I think. *I'm so glad they came to see us.*

All in all, over twenty people show up for that performance. We do it in shock.

Only after it's over do the girls tell me the Bible study in question was the one we wrote last year in British Columbia and disseminate via email. Without our knowing anything about it, this group has been doing it together as their women's small group study through their church.

The evening feels like a gift from God, a reminder that yes, the work matters; yes, the words matter; they go out into the world like seeds and they make a difference even without us being present, or knowing anything about it.

It's a touch from heaven that says *I see you.*

I honor you.

Keep going.

Camp ends. We have one day to gather our wits, debrief, rest. And then we hit the road for Ottawa and two more weeks of teaching.

LOST?

IN OTTAWA I DECIDE to trek around Mud Lake again.

I've never forgotten the magic of discovering this little spot in the woods last year, and the image I received from the Lord there—*fat cows and lean cows*—is still vivid, relevant, and fear-inducing.

I'm hoping that in going out in the morning and hiking around the lake, I can clear my head, pray, and hear from the Lord again. The last month and a half have been a fog of constant mental turmoil. I desperately need to come up for air and gain some clarity.

So I pull on my hiking boots, fill a water bottle, and head out around 7 a.m., having failed to talk anyone into coming with me and not really minding. It's hot and humid outside, with the typical sticky air of an Ontario summer, but already some of the woods are showing signs of the slanting light as leaves start to turn color and dry up, preparing to drop off for the long winter ahead.

I learned several years ago that trees don't just drop their leaves as a matter of course, as programmed into the DNA of this or that species. They do it by choice, as a response to the change in the light. As the north tips away from the sun and the light begins to weaken and the days grow shorter, the trees face diminishing returns in their efforts to photosynthesize. At the same time, leaves give them many extra surfaces that are vulnerable to damage from wind, rain, animals, and disease. So sometime in the fall, they make the decision to drop their leaves, minimize damage, and conserve their energy—hunkering down, essentially, for the winter months. Here, that means November through April or May.

It's a hard life for trees. As it can be, sometimes, for those of us who hike the trails beneath them.

My own hike starts out well. I recognize the path, and although it's been damaged a little by recent flooding, I'm able to walk it without much trouble. Until I reach a fork.

One trail goes right, toward the lake. The other goes left, into the trees.

I vaguely remember this fork in the road from last year, and what I recall is that I took the left fork—wanting to stay close to the water, and also figuring this must be the path that follows the shore of the lake, as I want to do—and it ended after a little while out on a little promontory overlooking the water. I had to backtrack and come back, then take the fork into the trees.

But it wasn't a bad detour, and the view was pretty, so I decide to do it again.

The path is more overgrown this year, but I've got hiking pants; and although the whole thing is sweltering in mud—also different from last year—I've got boots. The trek is hard work and won't leave my mind free enough to pray, but this will be a short detour and then I'll come back to the main route. I'm grateful for good equipment. In running shoes and jeans this would be a terrible idea.

In fact, it's not an especially good idea anyway—or at least, as I swipe away branches and try to avoid deep mud holes, it's not what I remember. I pass the point where I thought a promontory was and find that the path continues forward, and now I have a conundrum.

Turn back now?

Or keep going?

The path has changed since last year. It would seem that someone has forged a new one, and from the degree to which it's been trampled down, many someones must have walked it. It stretches much further than the old path did, and so I tell myself it must rejoin the main path after all. Someone has created a loop.

So many people have walked this path that it must go somewhere.

So I push forward, mosquitos and mud and branches and all, and I wish I'd taken the main path back at the fork. But I didn't know this would keep going so far, and now that I'm here, I don't want to waste the time going back through the undergrowth. I want to get back on a clear path, where I can see where I'm going, where I can let my mind wander so I can focus and I can pray.

(Wandering in order to focus does make scientific sense. "Daydreaming in the absence of distractions activates the brain's default-mode network," says the BBC. "Giving free rein to a wandering mind not only helps with focus in the long term but strengthens your sense of both yourself and others.")

I convince myself that I've gone too far to make turning around reasonable. Surely this will rejoin the main track at any time, and I won't be forced to retread the whole misbegotten way again.

I'm wrong.

I finally come out on a little piece of land jutting into the water, a dead-end.

I'm going to have to turn around and retrace my steps.

I've wasted a lot of time.

Frustrated and downcast as I pick my way back, I realize I'm not even going to be able to finish my circuit of the lake. My belief that *this path must lead somewhere; so many people have taken it!* has cost me too much time, and at this point I just need to retrace all my steps and go home. I need a shower, besides. And to clean my boots.

In the shower I notice a patch of poison ivy on my foot.

I've learned some things about paths. At least I think I have.

> **1.** If you're on a wrong path, don't just keep going because you don't want to retrace your steps. Go back to the last place where you knew where you were.
>
> **2.** The sooner you turn around, the better.
>
> **3.** Don't assume that just because others have taken a path, they knew where they were going—or even that the path was made with intention.

I argue a lot with God on the way home. I can see the

metaphor, but not how it applies. And what if you're pioneering? What if there is no clear path? The pioneers, I remind him, had guides. Lewis and Clark had guides. The paths were there. Ancient paths were there.

I need to find my path again, but I'm lost in the woods and for the life of me, I don't know how.

SICK

AS OUR SECOND WEEK in Ottawa begins, I wrap up a teaching session in the morning and go out with Mercy and our friend Natalie to shop a little (well, to window-shop ... I am too broke to actually buy anything). It's a nice day, very warm, and sunny. We head for an outlet mall and wander in and out of a few shops, when I notice I don't feel especially well. My stomach hurts a bit.

A few minutes later, I'm feeling a pressing need to lie down, and I touch Mercy's shoulder and let her know I'm going outside to find a bench.

I find a spot in the sun and stretch out. But within minutes my whole body aches, and I'm shaking with chills.

Realizing I can't just lie here in public like this, I force myself to my feet and stagger the whole way back to the car, where I lie on the back seat in the sun because I'm so chilled I can't warm up. Part of me knows this is a bad idea and maybe even dangerous; that's it gotten downright hot outside, and I'm lying inside a black car in full sun with the windows only slightly cracked for ventilation. But I can't stop shaking—convulsing—and I know I'm very, very sick.

As I curl up in the sun and try to still the shaking, oppressive fear settles in. Fear that my ICD will react to whatever is happening in my body by misfiring. Fear that I'll actually have a heart attack. Fear that my heart is causing this somehow.

Fear that I'm being attacked, and the attacker is going to win.

I wonder if I'm going to die.

I close my eyes, remind myself out loud, again and again, that the Lord is my shepherd. Though I walk through the valley of the shadow of death, I will fear no evil, for he is with me. His rod and his staff, they comfort me.

I memorized it as a child, this psalm, in the King James English I grew up reading.

Thou preparest a table before me in the presence of mine enemies. Thou anointest my head with oil. My cup runneth over. Surely, goodness and mercy shall follow me all the days of my life, and I will dwell in the house of the Lord forever.

After an hour Mercy and Natalie come back to the car, and my chills subside. The fever remains. We go back to the house where we're staying with friends, and I crawl into the little bed in a corner of the basement where I'm staying.

I get out of bed in the morning just long enough to teach, then come back and spend most of the day in and out of fever, in and out of sleep.

That remains the pattern for the rest of the week. The worst of the fever breaks after a day or two, but I am exhausted, aching, and unable to function on anything like a normal level until camp is over and it's time to go home.

DIAGNOSED

WITH CAMP SEASON BEHIND US, Carolyn and I return home. Mercy is gone; flown back to North Carolina straight from Ottawa. I miss her as I always do when she's gone, and we're leaving behind friends in Ottawa too—always bittersweet. But it's good to go home. It's good to feel that the only demands I have on me now are somehow saving the business, the work, the house, everything.

September brings another mortgage payment with it, and I marvel that I can pay it. I'm not sure how it's possible. I'm not sure, looking back, how we are still afloat at all. Income has been on a precipitous decline since May; how, at the beginning of fall, we are still solvent is somewhere beyond miraculous.

The panic is over now. It's giving way to a sense of deep and gritty tiredness, but with that, the sense that I can go on—I can keep putting one foot in front of the other; and if I can't, overnight, solve the problems and find the answers, that will be okay.

Home means reconnecting with friends. Taking a walk with a friend from church, I share about getting sick again and mention that it's become a pattern. I'm not really one to go to the doctor, and somehow it's never even occurred to me until now that I ought to. I've seen these attacks as related to exhaustion, to stress, to spiritual warfare, to my body "just not being the same" after the cardiac arrest. But as we talk I say: "If it happens again and we're home, not traveling, I think I'm going to go in."

Two weeks later, I wake up in the middle of the night in pain and shaking with violent chills.

I wake Carolyn and ask her to pray for me, and she gets up and putters around making tea and helping me get comfortable until the chills finally subside.

In the morning we go to the hospital.

The chills are gone now, but I'm sure I'm still feverish. That's confirmed when the ER doesn't send me home; they give me one of the few beds in our tiny small-town hospital where I can wait for a doctor, along with Tylenol to bring the fever down. Chills set in again, and Carolyn finds me blankets from a warmer and helps me get calm.

The nurse objects at first—I'm not supposed to get too warm when I already have a fever—but when she hears my teeth chattering she has mercy on me and helps Carolyn pile on a few more.

When the doctor arrives he asks some obvious questions, the answers to all of which are unsatisfactory. They've taken blood, but we have to wait for results. He decides to do just a basic physical, and as soon as he starts to poke around my abdomen he stops, pushes on something, and says, "What is that?"

I'm not entirely sure what he means, except that I am swollen, like I have been almost perpetually for a couple of years now.

"Um," I said, "well, I tend to be kind of bloated."

"That's not bloating," he says. "That's like if you were pregnant. Could you be pregnant?"

No. Definitely not.

"You're not bloated," he says again. "There's something in there. I don't want you going home until we find out what it is."

Our hospital is very small, and not well equipped. It turns out ultrasound won't be possible for another day.

My blood pressure is a little low, so he orders a bag of

saline solution to raise it. Instead of going up, it plummets.

"I'm not really happy with the way you're reacting," he tells me after another hour or so, "and we can't do a scan here. I'm going to send you to Welland by ambulance."

An hour later I'm loaded on a stretcher and headed out to the ambulance. Carolyn has already called Welland in advance, alerting our church family that we're coming. She'll drive in behind the ambulance. I still feel terrible but can think clearly enough to make the best of it: I've never ridden in an ambulance while conscious. I can add this to my list of interesting life experiences.

It gets even more interesting, though, when I actually settle into the back of the ambulance with a paramedic beside me typing symptoms into a laptop—because with every fiber of my being I know I've done this before. I remember it, even though I don't. I have absolutely no conscious memory of riding in the ambulance after being brought back from cardiac arrest; I was not awake at the time. Yet absolutely everything about lying here is familiar to me. I've seen it all before: the shelves of medical equipment behind Plexiglas on one side of me, the ceiling, the paramedic.

They say that cellular memory is a real thing; that every cell in your body is imprinted by things that happen to you, especially traumatic things. I don't feel fear as the trek to Welland begins and the light of the setting sun comes through the small window in the back. But I do feel memory. It's a strange and almost eerie feeling.

In Welland I wait for a while on a stretcher in a back hallway for a bed to come available in the ER. Carolyn can't come back here, but Lorraine, a dear friend from church who happens to have a special access badge as a spiritual care practitioner in the hospital, can. She brings me a bottle of water, prayer, and a loving touch. "You're so hot," she says.

Once moved into the ER, more church friends and family come back to see me, two at a time. Apparently there's quite a party in the lobby. I'm deeply blessed.

The first doctor's proclamation, "There's something in there," has clicked. I know what it is. It's a fibroid. I laugh over this, the sudden "oh, of course"—I've had symptoms of this thing for years now, primarily the visible and palpable swelling, so extreme that if I lie on my stomach I feel like I'm lying on a bowling ball at times. And all this time I've told myself it was bloating. But years ago I had an ovarian cyst that burst, and in the series of ultrasounds done to make sure nothing too serious was happening, the doctors discovered a fibroid.

Back then, a decade or so ago, it was small, nothing to be concerned about.

A fibroid is a benign uterine tumor. About 70 percent of women get them. In most cases they're asymptomatic and never cause problems. The nurse at the time told me it could cause a problem down the road if I wanted to get pregnant, but we could cross that bridge if we came to it.

But fibroids can grow, and apparently this one has.

There is no reason a fibroid should cause attacks of fever, so its discovery seems like little more than a rabbit trail at the moment. I and most of my friends are more concerned about the possibility of something being wrong with my heart, or even that my body might be reacting badly to the ICD—treating it as a foreign object, attacking it in some kind of autoimmune response. None of the doctors seem to think this is likely, although they do acknowledge it's an outside possibility.

I go in for a CT scan of my abdomen. An hour later the results are back: large uterine mass, eleven by fourteen centimeters (about the size of a cantaloupe), probably a fibroid. The scan can't identify it for certain.

Bloodwork finally comes back. It's all clear.

I still have a fever, but there's no sign of infection anywhere.

I remain in the ER until 3:30 in the morning. Lorraine takes Carolyn home and puts her to bed in their spare room; her husband, Jim, stays with me—sitting by my bed until finally the doctor says, "We still don't know what's causing this, but the fever has broken and you're getting better. It's up to you: you can stay here while we continue to run more tests, or you can go home and come back as an outpatient, and we'll do more tests out of our clinic."

I opt for the second choice and finally go home.

Two weeks later, the outpatient clinic has put the pieces together. It is, in fact, the fibroid causing the fevers—in a roundabout way. It's putting so much pressure on my bladder that it's causing fluid to back up into my kidneys. They found a minor bladder infection—the kind that's extremely common and isn't usually even treated—but with infection moving into my kidneys, my whole body is freaking out.

And things are definitely more serious than a bladder infection. The fibroid is still growing, and at this point it is already partially blocking my ureters, the tubes that run from kidneys to bladder. If growth continues it will cut them off completely, and my kidneys will develop a severe infection and fail.

"It has to come out," the doctor says.

RELIEF

EVEN KNOWING there is something really wrong in your body, even knowing you now have a major surgery on the horizon, and even knowing it will likely have life-changing ramifications—almost certainly this is going to mean I will be unable to have children in the future—there is tremendous relief to fitting a piece into a puzzle.

I've been growing something, sustaining and feeding it, for three years. It has affected my hormones and my energy. I know now it hasn't just been the stress of financial pressure that made me unable to think clearly. I know it wasn't just coming down with severe fevers regularly that has made me so constantly, consistently tired.

It's mid-September, and my surgery isn't scheduled until late January.

Just before the diagnosis, my symptoms had worsened considerably. Every month, the fibroid grows. Suddenly

I'm dealing with a multitude of new symptoms, from trouble with digestion to needing the bathroom constantly to a limp in my left leg where it seems a nerve is getting pinched. I need more and more and more sleep, and as winter sets in, it begins to feel impossible to really wake up. I can't manage a full workday. I struggle to think clearly. I'm in pain a majority of the time.

Twice symptoms lead to hyperventilating and tachycardia. It feels like I'm having a heart attack.

But I'm relieved.

Because there's an answer and an end on the horizon.

I want to be well again. I'm daring to dream that my health can return to what it was before all of this, not just find a level of coping that is more functional than what I'm experiencing right now. With that, I look forward to feeling *capable* again. I recognize that part of the panic and fear around work has been that I've actually felt incapable of working full-time hours, meeting deadlines, doing client work. I have felt like I could not do it without a severe breakdown. After all, that's been the pattern. Take on a lot, end up in bed for weeks.

This can change.

I just have to make it through to January.

NEW OPPORTUNITY

IN LATE SEPTEMBER, an opportunity for a new type of client work opens up. It's writing (not editing); it has the potential to pay really well. It comes out of absolutely nowhere: an old colleague with whom I haven't spoken in years emails me about it.

It feels like movement in the wrong direction—going backwards in some respects. It's back to a "lean cow" model; back to trading time for dollars; back to focusing on the work and priorities of others and not on the work and priorities burning in my heart.

But I pray, and I feel I'm to accept it.

It's provision for the moment, not forever. It will pay some bills and let me get my feet back under myself, as I need so desperately to do.

It renews some hope and lights a path of possibility. It

reminds me, most of all, that things can change dramatically overnight, even without my having figured anything out or caused something great to happen.

So I say yes.

ALL GOD'S PEOPLE SAY HMMM

THROUGHOUT THIS JOURNEY, my faith community means more than I can possibly express. There's Mercy and Carolyn, of course. They've journeyed beside me for years.

But now there's my church family too. We came to Wellspring for the first time just a few months prior to my cardiac arrest, and when that happened, we didn't yet have any real relationships within the church—we'd spend almost all of the time from discovering Wellspring to September 2014 on the road, doing ministry for 1:11.

Since then so much has changed. We've been adopted. I've been adopted. The party in the waiting room at the hospital reflects that better than anything. Every day, every week, I get a message from someone with a word of encouragement. With a prophetic word or picture (usually having to do with abundance, blessing, rain, a promise of expanded territory, encouragement to keep going). Church family come over to pray with me. They go for walks on the beach with me and ask penetrating questions just to check on my heart and mind and make sure I'm in a good place. They offer insight and hugs and groceries.

("You would tell us if you couldn't buy food, right? Don't you dare ever go hungry. Please know that if you're ever really in a bind, you can call on anyone in this room.")

One night at prayer meeting when I'm feeling particularly beaten down, my friend Jim leads us in praying against the spirit of fear. Then he says, "Tonight we're going to do something a little different. I want you to break into groups of two or three, and I want you to confess your fears to one another, and I want you to pray for one another."

Our prayer meetings don't usually have a huge turnout, and my little group of three consists of myself, my little sister Keturah (who's been living with Carolyn and me on and off for a couple of months), and Ralph, one of our elders. We go around the circle and pray for one another, and of course, my prayer request is about my work—my finances—the twin giants of needing to pay the bills and needing to find a way to stay true to my calling.

There's another little fear I don't confess: the fear that one of these days someone older and wiser is going to say, "Look, Rachel, we know you meant well, but you need to give up. This whole thing is off base, and it's clear it's not going to work. We think you should quit now and go back to working a real job before everything gets even more out of hand than it already is."

But Ralph doesn't say that. Instead, he tells me a story of a time when he was young and needed to pass an exam in order to enter a career he wanted. He knew the material, but because of challenges with reading comprehension, he didn't pass. He went home determined to give up on his dream and settle for something less.

The next day, two men from his chosen profession made a three-hour trek out to see him. Ralph fixes his gaze on me as he tells the story. "They sat me down and said, 'We believe in you. We know you can do this.'"

With that, he launches into prayer for me. "Show her, Lord," he declares, "that there's no going back now! She's in too deep; the only way is forward with you."

As I leave prayer meeting that night, another friend slips me five bucks for tea and a donut on the forty-minute drive home. I'm encouraged. I'm grateful.

My friend Diana and I like to characterize our church friends with a little slogan we made up: "And all God's people say *hmmm*." Within this body there's a sense of journeying together, studying and listening together, connecting dots and growing in the Spirit together. That sense means less judgment, more curiosity, and more willingness to hang in there for a promised outcome.

It's exactly the kind of support I need.

BINGING ON NETFLIX AS A TOOL FOR CREATIVITY AND SELF-REFLECTION

QUITE SOME TIME AGO, early in the year while I still had money and anticipated a continuing income from my book sales, I bought a ticket for Jeff Walker's Launch Conference in Dallas, Texas. The conference dates are mid-October. My airfare is paid, no hope of a real refund on that, and I can stay with Becky and Kevin in Arlington.

But I'm torn about going. I'm about to start work for my new writing client, and the idea of juggling client deadlines with conference attendance is stressful all by itself. Even without that, the truth is, my mind at the moment feels like such a pressure cooker that I'm fairly sure adding anything new will only increase the mush. On the one hand I think the conference could be excellent for stimulating new ideas and making contacts; on the other, I already know so much that I'm not really implementing yet.

Maybe, rather than take in more information, I just need to act on something strategic that I already know.

Beyond that, though, is a deeper reason I don't want to go. Whether the conference itself would benefit me or be a wash feels like a 50/50 question right now; there's no real way to know without going. But I know myself well enough to know that networking events rarely bear any real fruit in my business or in my life. And mostly, I'm exhausted.

These last few months have been brutal. Emotionally, spiritually, physically, mentally. I'm at a point where I need twelve hours of sleep a night just to function, and even then I'm not really firing on all cylinders. The idea of arranging transportation to and from the conference, or of grabbing dinner out with a few colleagues, makes me want to curl up and hide.

I need new life in my business, yes. But more than that, I really, really need a rest.

I chat with Becky about it one night. "What I really want to do," I tell her, "is come to your house, drink coffee on your front porch, and take naps on your couch when I'm not doing client work." And she tells me, "You know, I think there's nothing wrong with that."

And I am grateful.

For her understanding. For the lack of condemnation.

For the chance just to catch my breath.

I email Jeff Walker's team and explain my situation: that I know we are way past a reasonable refund date, and that I'm fairly sure refunds weren't available anyway (I bought my ticket at an early bird discount), but that I'm sick and facing financial hardship and if they could possibly refund me, I would be ever so grateful.

They promptly write back, graciously and sympathetically, with a full refund.

And I am grateful for that too.

In early October I fly to Dallas. It's beautiful and warm here, just like it was in March when I last came—when I was feeling free for the first time, building out my new blog and the upgraded Lifetime Readers Club and studying how to launch. Something about being in someone else's home allows a load to roll off, like I can be a child here. It helps that although Becky is younger than me by a year, she's always sort of taken care of me. When we were kids most people assumed she was the older sister. I take a deep breath of Texas air under the trees and watch a lizard dart away from the back door, and I'm glad I came and that I came intending to rest.

The next day I wake up with a monstrous respiratory infection. Sore throat, deep chest, hacking stuff up. Feverish and achy and tired.

I never used to get sick. I had the world's best immune system, inherited from my mother. No one in the family ever got sick except Becky, who inherited *her* immune system from the Thomson side of the family and thought it was outrageously unfair. But over the last few years my own ability to withstand infection has dropped ever further and further down, until now it seems like I spend more time unwell, either vaguely or fully, than I do in anything resembling good health.

There is another twist in the plot of my Texas visit: I hoped to begin working for my new client at eight hours a day, which would allow me to start pulling my feet back under me. But it turns out they have a multi-person review process for writing which moves quite slowly, and as a result, I don't really have work yet.

On the one hand, I know that's bad. Bills are still going to come due, and I don't have a way to pay them beyond the few royalties that are still coming in, month by month, without my needing to work for them—my homebuilt "fat cow" economy in action, if drastically scaled down. That money comes in month after month with a lode-star pull: *This is the way, walk ye in it.* I would, in a heartbeat, if I could escape the chokehold that's currently got my finances locked down and unable to reach their potential.

On the other hand, I'm sick, I'm tired, and I really don't want to work anyway.

So I take the opportunity *just* to rest with gladness. I spend a lot of time on the front porch, drinking coffee from the Keurig (the height of luxury) and listening to sermons from a free online seminary course I'm taking ("Biblical Theology" by G.K. Beale, on inaugurated eschatology and the use of the Old Testament in the New). I go for leisurely walks through the old country club neighborhood where my sister and brother-in-law live with his parents. I watch *Parks and Recreation* with Becky.

I sleep a lot.

Bits of work come in, an hour here and there. I'm working eight hours a week rather than eight a day. Again, this is bad. But again, I'm grateful.

How my bills have been paid since May, how I've never missed a mortgage payment, how I've had tight weeks where I couldn't pay certain bills but they got paid off eventually ... I don't really know how this has happened. It seems to me that quiet miracles are working in my life, and God is keeping his promises—not only to feed me, and to notice if I fall, but to catch me on a grander scale and keep me going forward when I don't think I can.

Kevin has Netflix, and I sign in on my laptop one night when I'm feeling particularly terrible and explore the fabled US site, home of many many more movies and shows than its Canadian counterpart. Not much appeals. I'm a fantasy fan; in the world of fiction, I don't like drama, and I dislike anything that strongly resembles real life. Unfortunately, most fantasy is either terribly cheesy or *Lord of the Rings,* and I'm not really up for that much commitment.

Cinema and TV in any form are not big parts of my life. I go to see every Marvel movie religiously (except the ones put out by Fox), but other than that and the occasional cartoon I'm not especially interested. I poke around for a while, being disappointed by the first few minutes of several DC series and then a particularly terrible *Dragonheart* movie, and then when it's very late and I really, truly ought to be going to bed, I watch an episode of *The Shannara Chronicles* instead.

When this show came out, I tried to watch the first episode through some bootleg site that we could access in Canada, but either my computer or the network connection were so bad that it was like watching a flipbook with stops. I gave up, though not before deciding I didn't much care for the series.

This time the show actually flows from frame to frame properly, which means I have time to get past the annoying parts (still annoying) and grow interested in the story.

The series is based on Terry Brooks's Shannara books,

of which there are dozens. They are not great literature by any means, but *The Sword of Shannara* was the first grown-up fantasy book I ever read, and it did loads to shape my imagination, my understanding of the genre, and my deep fascination with it.

(*The Sword of Shannara* is also such a play-by-play Tolkien knock-off that when I read *Lord of the Rings* for the first time, years later, I recognized multiple characters, scenes, and plot twists from Brooks. And then promptly reused them all in my own earliest fantasy. That *Sword* was ever published at all is a fascinating story and beyond the scope of this memoir, but Brooks proved himself to be a capable and original writer after that.)

I stay up watching *Shannara* until 2 a.m. I'm surprised by delight, by enjoying something I didn't expect to enjoy. I'm pulled along by the cliff-hangers and the edgy music and characters I care about. I wake up and finish it the next morning, luxuriating in not having work, even in the freedom of being sick and not at home and not having to do a single thing.

I don't recommend binge-watching Netflix as a lifestyle. I'm not a TV fan in general.

But somehow, watching 480 straight hours of a miniseries resets something in my brain.

The same night I finish watching *Shannara*, I sit down

and start Seeds again, from scratch. It's been stuck since early August, and now I know why. I had the tone wrong. It was too serious, too self-aware. It needed exactly what *Shannara* gave me: a renewed sense of adventure, of joy, of mystery, and of good old-fashioned camp.

I throw out all one hundred previously written pages and start from scratch, and that evening I write thirty pages and the next day I write another forty or so. And it's fun. It's play.

I haven't played like this in a *long* time.

Years and years of writer's block have finally broken.

I go home and I keep watching Netflix. I find a sci-fi show (*Dark Matter*, seasons 1 and 2), and then an Australian buddy flick about two women fugitives on the run *(Wanted)*. Between bouts of work and writing, I lie on the couch sick and watch hours at a time. And it all goes to good use. I write to the soundtrack and related music from *Shannara*, thanks to an MTV playlist on Spotify. *Dark Matter* pushes me through plot twists. *Wanted* has me psychoanalyzing myself and gives me one of my favorite ever pictures of what it means to take up a cross and follow Jesus: it's a journey of companionship, a choosing to suffer for the sake of sharing a load and in the process being transformed and set free.

All three shows also make me realize how deeply friendship matters to me and how much I care about justice and vindication.

Shannara also speaks to me about redemptive suffering and why suffering makes sense in an era of clashing kingdoms. The Christian life is much like the journey of the long-suffering companions in Terry Brooks's novel and like the journey of Frodo Baggins before it: it is redemptive, it is beleaguered, and it is meant to save the very same world that so often attacks and oppresses out of ignorance, corruption, and sin.

I realize that to an absurd degree, this is the picture of life that resonates with me: that of a small band of companions making their way through a dark and fierce world, carrying a mandate and a mission that will save that world, often while misunderstood and opposed by everyone around them.

I journal on them, these hours and hours of drama watching. But they all come to an end.

Dark Matter and *Shannara* both have further seasons, but both go in moral directions I don't want to follow.

Wanted will have a third season, but it's got to be filmed (in Australia, no less) and likely won't appear on Netflix for another year or so. I poke around at other shows, but nothing garners my interest.

The season of binge-watching has ended. It's done me a tremendous and completely unexpected favor. Sicker than I've ever been, I am also now more creatively alive than I've been in years.

EVERYTHING IS CAPABLE OF CHANGING IN AN INSTANT

PART OF THE MENTAL BATTLE of this year has been the need to understand and embrace a truth: that everything can change in an instant, and sometimes it does.

The whole thrust of this season, the message the enemy is trying to bludgeon into my head, is *You're stuck here, nothing ever changes, it's hopeless and it's never going to shift.*

Miracles don't happen; that's what this year wants me to believe.

And yet, that's not true.

I didn't know, when I surfed my way onto an MTV fantasy show on Netflix one night, that two days later I would have broken through a decade of writer's block and be furiously writing my new novel with true joy.

A writing client can show up out of thin air.

An idea can change the landscape of possibility.

So many of the really big changes, the forks in the road, they happen unexpectedly, in an instant.

Yet there's also this truth: that if you aren't on the path in the first place, you won't come across the miracle moments. It's like they say about "overnight" successes: they usually have decades of work behind them. You can't control whether you're in the right place at the right time, except that you *can* ensure you're in the right place, or as close to it as possible.

This is something I recognized last summer, when I first realized the kind of impact scaling my Facebook ads could have. I felt, deep down, like it couldn't possibly be this easy. It felt morally *wrong* for it to be so easy. Nobody can just make an ad, run it, and two months later be financially free. It doesn't work like that.

Until I realized that before I ever started running profitable ads, I wrote and released thirty titles on Amazon.

My overnight success wasn't overnight either. It took decades of dogged determination, work, and investment, in myself and in my books.

Twin truths:

Everything is capable of changing in a moment.
But in order to experience the change, you've got to be in its way.

YOUR KINGDOM CALLING REBORN

LATE OCTOBER, and Mercy comes up for a season of ministry. We've booked several performances for the 1:11 team in the Greater Toronto Area. I'm battling chronic symptoms that are getting worse by the month, and November—when our Christmas season will officially begin—is a little terrifying to contemplate. We always have a number of performances around the holidays, which means I'll be doing a lot of speaking, and Mercy leaves just before American Thanksgiving and won't be able to spell me off.

My financial problems aren't fixed, but I'm calmer about it now. I'm taking more contract work, working hard now on *Seeds*, and keeping my eyes open for opportunity—for places in the path where instant and unexpected changes could happen.

I map out products I have already created that have

the potential to earn money for me if I'm faithful to do promotional pushes (sort of mini-launches) for them. One of these is *Your Kingdom Calling*. Enough time has passed by now that I'm not so raw about the failed launch, and there is this truth that keeps cropping up: I really and truly believe people need the concepts in the course. It's just not right for it to sit on my hard drive and do nothing either for me or for others.

I decide I'm going to do another launch for YKC. I want to add something new to the mix, though, so I hit upon an idea: I'll take the transcripts for the free workshop and polish them into an ebook, then release it on Amazon for free to reach more people.

I hire my sister to make a quick and inexpensive cover for me, spend a couple of days creating the book, and release it without fanfare. I let my list know it's there.

I'm surprised by the number of downloads it gets—several hundred.

This is a good reminder of something I've slowly been learning: just because I've put something into the world and even promoted it heavily for a little while does NOT mean everyone in my audience has paid attention to it.

For many people, the thing you're tired of is still brand new.

So if it's worthwhile, if it's got value in itself, it's worth continuing to promote.

I get a few days with downloads in the hundreds and I'm very pleased.

About a week later, we're leaving the house for a Saturday night performance in Toronto. I feel good as I'm getting dressed and having my coffee, until our ride arrives—at which point I am suddenly and debilitatingly ill.

I sit down at the dining room table and let everyone else load the vehicles and do the prep work while I just try to stay vertical. Looking for distraction, I grab my laptop and check my Kindle stats for the morning.

That's when I notice *Your Kingdom Calling* downloads are in the thousands.

In the next three days, my little ebook hits #2 in the entire Religion & Spirituality category on Amazon—a category with well over 100,000 titles in its ranks.

I don't know why.

I'm awestruck.

And thankful.

Everything is capable of changing overnight.

PIVOT

ONE OF THE HARDER DYNAMICS of this season is that everything important to me feels like it has to be shoehorned into the edges of my days.

Psalm 66:10–12 is a good picture of how I feel about life in general right now:

> For You, God, tested us;
> You refined us as silver is refined.
> You lured us into a trap;
> You placed burdens on our backs.
> You let men ride over our heads;
> we went through fire and water,
> but You brought us out to abundance.

Mind you, I'm not feeling that last bit yet … we're still firmly in the "men riding over our heads" stage.

Revelatory Creative matters. This journey through the gospel of Matthew, which at this point I estimate is roughly equivalent to a four-hundred-page book and is likely to end between eight hundred and a thousand pages by the time I've finished it, matters to people—this I know, for they have told me. Besides which, it matters to me.

It's also a great deal of work. The articles I write for it run about 1200 words, and to do them properly means spending time studying and praying first. I *can* whip off 1200 words with no prior preparation. On the one hand this is only possible because I've been reading and studying the Bible in depth since I was a teenager; it's the fruit of years of work—so I don't want to downplay that. On the other hand, I don't want to get cavalier about teaching the Scriptures, and I don't want to spend all my time relaying old revelation instead of seeking out something fresh and new.

About halfway through my relaunch of *Your Kingdom Calling*, during which I'm running the workshop again and promoting the new ebook, I decide that when I reach the "selling" part of the promotion, I'm not going to sell YKC. I'm going to invite readers to sponsor my blog, and if they do, I'm going to give them *Your Kingdom Calling* for free.

I've been so ambivalent about asking people for support. I've wanted to keep things really clean—I sell you something, you give me money. Support is a messier model in some ways. But the truth is, I can't put the time I need to put into the blog, to do it really right, unless it can somehow cover my bills during the hours I'm working on it.

So I shift gears. I offer sponsorships and YKC as a bonus. In that week I raise about $400 a month, and I find that I can breathe again, at least in this area. It's enough to cover an hour of study and an hour of writing each week, and that's enough to enable me to write the blog properly.

It's hard for me to open myself up to "help." I've come to recognize that I'm independent, almost fiercely so, and I don't think anyone owes me money for doing what I'm called to do.

But this year has made me realize anew that my calling isn't just for me. It's truly for others. It's truly for the kingdom.

So maybe it's okay for others to help. Maybe it's okay for people to support what I do, just because they believe in it and benefit from it, and not because I've "earned" it.

FEARLESS REBORN

BACK IN THE SUMMER a friend of ours, Josh Gilman of the anti-porn organization Strength to Fight, did an interview with the 700 Club Canada. It's been a few years since 1:11 Ministries was on TV, and we'd like to book a *Fearless* (the show) tour across Canada in the new year ... besides which, our grand plan to give away 10,000 free copies of *Fearless* (the book) is just barely above a stall at 2500-ish copies.

We can use some fresh fuel on the fire.

So we connect with the 700 Club through Josh, chat with their booking agent over the phone, and set up a pair of interviews—Mercy and I—to talk about our personal "fearless" stories and let people know about our book and our ministry alike.

The interviews are scheduled for November, but they won't air until January 2018. We dress up, me borrowing a pair of jeans from Mercy because mine are stretched out, I can't afford new ones, and for the most part I haven't worn jeans since August. Painful and distended is a real thing. I'm most comfortable now in stretchy pants or maternity clothes, and have started favoring baggy shirts because I truly do look pregnant, and I really don't want to start any rumors.

Getting ready for the interviews, I hit a new low. I hate feeling uncomfortable in anything I wear and worrying that if my jeans are tight they'll make my symptoms flare up worse. I wish I had a haircut, but I can't afford one. I haven't worn makeup for months because I developed a problem with dry eyes last year that causes my eyes to sting and water horribly when they get irritated—which they do when mascara is involved. I'm supposed to prep my own makeup and have the 700 Club's makeup artist just touch it up, but I don't currently own any. I feel tired, worn down, worn out, and drab, and honestly, I don't feel super up to talking about fear. I want to stay in bed and curl up with a hot cup of cocoa and a mini-series, and I don't want to be responsible, adult, or famous.

I'm going to go on TV anyway. I'm going to be a big girl, and talk about fear, and talk about holiness—which to me is a self-identity, a way of understanding your place in this world: that you belong to Jesus, that everything in life is about him. It's holiness that makes us fearless, or close to it; it's holiness that makes everything but Jesus irrelevant. Even if it's building a business, or crafting a career, or stopping a financial ship from going down in a burning cataclysm.

Then again, maybe holiness is precisely what makes those things relevant, if they are being done for the Lord and in the service of his kingdom.

I do know that this isn't actually likely to make me famous. Unless it's Oprah, the actual reach and impact of traditional media is pretty limited—and I've been around long enough to know that from personal experience as well as hearsay.

We drive up to Hamilton together and find the studio on a little side street. It's cold and windy, and the back door's locked; a kind woman in a security uniform lets us in, and we stand in a lot of long cold concrete hallways and feel lost until we spot someone we can follow and make our way toward the voices of human beings.

Considering their influence and reach, 700 Club Canada is a comparatively small operation. Their green room is a down-to-earth affair. There's a counter with a coffee pot and packages of Costco muffins, and a few shelves with old books and DVDs—many of them clearly donated by past guests. Staffers are in and out: anchors, camera people, the social media manager. I like it here. I like how real it feels; how much it seems like a small crew of people truly working hard to do something meaningful and making something excellent with the resources they have.

The hair and makeup lady doesn't say anything about my total lack of a preliminary face; she compliments my cardigan and does a great job with my makeup. The anchors are over chatting with the lighting people, and pretty soon the chief anchorman, Brian Warren, strikes up a prayer and everyone, cast and crew, stops to pray together—for one another, for their families, for the shows they'll film today. He gives a short devotional. It's clear everyone is listening. These people are the real deal.

Shortly before I go up for my interview, Brian kicks off the workday on set by asking for the airing date of the episode we're about to film—"What day is it?"

When someone answers "January 4," he rings out, "Happy New Year!"

Happy New Year, two months early. Happy New Year, in November, in a year when the tide has been awfully slow in turning, and a thousand times over, it has seemed like everything was crashing to an end.

The New Year has always been a time of hope and forward-looking for me. Of planning, dreaming, goal-setting. This year, I hope it will also feel like a release—like an escape from what has become a year of crushing weight.

Surgery is coming in January.

New hope for finances has, maybe, already started taking hold.

I really need a resurrection.

It's November. And the New Year.

Happy New Year.

"I DON'T DOUBT YOU'LL FIGURE IT OUT."

WHEN YOU HAVE an online business, everybody advertises to you.

New ads show up in my Facebook feed one day. I like them. They're for "writepreneurs," and the company is called Grit and Grace. The ad that draws my attention is one that tells a story, of the entrepreneur in question—Kristina Voegele—and how her brother told her if she was going to write, she'd better get used to flipping hamburgers.

I've been on something of an information fast since October or so. With my panic subsided and contract work back on the table, time has been tight. So have energy and motivation. I've recognized my tendency to substitute learning for doing, so I've kept my schedule relatively clear of webinars and launch workshops and podcast episodes lately.

It's also possible I've gotten a little jaded.

But I click on this one and sign up for the webinar.

Lucky me, there's something broken in Kristina's automated email follow-up sequence: it doesn't give a date or time for the webinar. That gives me an excuse to write her and introduce myself and tell her I like what I see and want to make sure she doesn't spend money getting people signed up for her webinar only to have no one show up and see her offer.

I'm a little too familiar with that myself.

She writes back, I watch her webinar, and before you know it we're on the phone and enjoying each other's company. Kristina coaches writers, and she very generously listens to my sob story of how I built a list of 30,000 readers and made over $18,000 in a single month, only to have it all come crashing down through a cash flow crisis so bad it choked out all momentum and growth.

"You sound like you've been really shaken by that," she observes.

It's true. I mostly put on a brave face in public. I have striven to keep the faith—not just as a front, but truly. I've gone back and back and back to the Lord, back to promises, back to vision, back to dreaming, back to the belief that I am doing what I am called to do.

He confirms it. Regularly.

But I am more shaken and tattered than I like to admit to myself.

I tell her my next step is to finish my new novel and publish it. I've recently realized that all my old publishing success was built on backlist; I've never launched a book to an actual audience before. It could work. It could work well enough to get me back on my feet by the end of March.

"So what are you doing to cover the bills in the meantime?" she asks.

I don't really know. There's consulting. But I don't like consulting.

"Don't do it then," she says. "I feel like you should be making a course. I mean, you built a list of 17,000 people in a year! With Christian fiction! That's crazy!"

"Actually," I say with a smile, "I built a list of 30,000 people in three months."

"So all you need to do is find something those people want and make it for them. I don't doubt you're going to figure this out. I mean … you're really kind of badass."

That one keeps me smiling for weeks.

Seeds is inching toward completion. I'm thinking now about other things I could do. Surgery is coming.

But first Christmas.

And I'm grateful to feel hope.

A ROOM OF ONE'S OWN

THE ENTIRE FAMILY comes home for Christmas. I love my family, but that is a whole heaping lot of people in my parents' house. For years we were just the twelve of us plus Mom and Dad, but in the last five we've seen four new families created, and right now that includes five little grandchildren plus one due in April. (If you're doing the math and wondering how we jumped to five kids in five years with only four families … we started with twins.)

My parents live in a big, sprawling, one-time mansion where my father grew up. When his father acquired it, it was already old and run-down. These days it's literally falling to pieces. When it rains, bits of plaster drop off the ceiling onto the beds upstairs. There's usually something nesting in the attic. But it's home. There are a lot of memories here, two generations of them. I was born in the small apartment on one side where Dad has his office now, and I lived there, right next door to my grandparents and the younger set of aunts and uncles—Dad's the oldest of eight kids himself—for most of my childhood until we moved to California when I was twelve.

After Grandma passed away suddenly in 2003, Grandpa married again within eighteen months, and he invited my family to move in as he was moving out to live with his new wife, Gail, at her place in the country. I lived in the upstairs bedroom right over the stairs for several years before trekking east to take up semi-permanent residence in the Niagara region.

When I come home for the holidays, or for random visits, I still stay up in the room above the stairs. As is common in old homes, there's a grate in the floor so heat can rise. Heat rises; so does noise. The room directly beneath the grate is the dining room and is located directly off the front door and between the kitchen and living room, so it's the busiest and loudest part of the entire house. My parents still have seven kids at home, and they themselves stay constantly busy, with church people and neighborhood contacts and customers for their custom chocolate business coming and going at all hours.

This is lovely in its way, but it's not conducive to getting much writing done, especially when I really want to be with family the majority of the time, and those sweet and funny little twins (three-year-old girls) live right upstairs and make the best distractions ever.

If I had money, I would get myself a hotel room. My parents could use the extra space, and I could very much use an office. There is one more consideration as well: I've always been introverted, but my fluctuating health has made overstimulation a serious problem that's liable to take me out for a day or two if I don't get a break.

But I don't have money.

I struggle with the sense of helplessness and poverty this brings. I've been blessed all my adult life since coming back to Canada to make money—quite decent money. But that's changed now, and sometimes I feel like it's changing my identity along with it. Like I've gone from being someone with a measure of independence and agency to someone who's stuck and helpless, and literally sick and tired, someone who isn't always sure she'll ever be able to get back up.

It's a head game. I know that. I pray it off. Pray it down. Pray it around in circles.

One of the hardest parts is that I didn't just do this to myself by making poor decisions. I did it to myself by trying to obey God, and I still believe that's what I'm doing, and I'm hanging on with everything I've got to the faith that he will not let me down and that I will pull through.

Every time—*every time*—I have gone to him over the last year to pray about this, and that is multiple times daily, he has said the same.

That I didn't go wrong.

That he's got me.

That I'm going to pull through, and it's going to be okay.

But sometimes it's hard to believe.

Talking to Kristina helped. It reminded me that I know things, valuable things. That just because I tried to launch a course and it failed doesn't mean I can't try again and have it succeed. That client work isn't the ultimate answer, because what I learned all about this year is still completely valid: an online, communication-based business can be viable, can scale, and can be far more lucrative in the long run than any dollars-for-hours arrangement could ever be.

I've got a loose plan now, and I'm working toward it. I'll launch *Seeds* in January. I hope to make enough sales, driven by the momentum of my email list, to bring in $10,000 in time to pay the next tax bill in April. If I can do that, and in the meantime I can use client contracts to pay the bills from January to March, then by the end of March I can be free again. Amazon will keep selling books for a few months on autopilot thanks to its algorithms, and I'll have enough to put money back into ads and restore my fortunes.

It's not a foolproof plan by any means—for one thing, I have no real idea how well my launch will go, and last time I tried ads they didn't work—but it's possible. And right now that's all I need.

I sit on my sister's old bed in the room over the stairs, put on headphones, and try to write my novel and get some work done for clients in the midst of Christmas celebrations. Heat wafts up the stairs, so does the smell of coffee, and now and again an icy draft knifes in from the window—it's an old house, like I said.

I'm home for the better part of December. Work is tricky. I miss my first hoped-for Seeds deadline, and then my second. I spend a few days sick on the couch and miss an outing to see the Christmas lights with the family for that reason. Just as well; it's bitterly cold outside, and I'm not handling the chill well.

Becky and Kevin come up for the holidays but there isn't room for them in the homestead, so they get a room at the Hampton Inn just up the road.

"Hey," I mention one afternoon, "I was thinking maybe I could go work in the lobby at your hotel."

"Of course," Becky says. "You're welcome to go up and use the room too … I'll get you a key."

So on December 27, shortly after Christmas Day, I find myself seated in an armchair overlooking the snowy city from the seventeenth floor, soaking up the warmth of a room without drafts, sipping a coffee from the lobby. My nearly finished manuscript is spread all over the floor; I'm at the stage where I have to read it before I can go into the final push for the ending. It's quiet. Almost silent.

It feels good.

I turn on worship music and pray for a while. Pace the room and seek the presence of my God, the one who set me on this journey, the one who is faithful.

So faithful that although I don't have money, I do have a hotel room of my own.

So faithful that although I've been constantly sick, broke, and nearly paralyzed with a lack of clarity as to what to do next, I've nearly written a novel—my eighteenth.

My best.

I get the manuscript all read through, and before I head home, I listen to an mp3 I downloaded earlier from a podcast I don't listen to. It's about a method of goal-setting called the 90-Day Year; something I've heard of and recently reencountered and want to learn more about.

The new year—the real one—is just around the corner.

I was dreading goal-setting this year. But the podcast sparks new thoughts, new possibilities. I think I'll try it.

On December 31, back over the stairs in my parents' house, I write "The End" in Seeds.

I've done it.

I almost didn't think I could.

"I GOT THAT"

"HEY, I MIGHT COME see you at work," I tell my sister Naomi as she wraps a white knit scarf around her neck on her way out the door.

"Oh, you should!"

"Well, I want to. I'd like to get some work done there." But then again … "I maybe shouldn't though, because I don't really have money for coffee." Darn external processing.

Naomi works at Anchor Coffee, a local coffee shop privately owned by a young Christian couple who are trying to serve God with aromatic beans. It works for me.

"Just come by, I'll treat you," Naomi says.

I'm not one to turn down an offer like that. Late that afternoon I drive across town to Walkerville, Windsor's old and charming west side, where there's a whole little renaissance of restaurants and shops and artsy places going on. Naomi buys me a latte and introduces me to her boss, Kyle. I set myself up in a corner right in front of the floor-length windows that front the shop and get busy editing for a client—a book about quantum physics, which is strangely therapeutic and just about my speed.

It's a good place. Laughter wafts out of the kitchen, where Naomi's working. Her boyfriend, James, arrives to pick her up, and I bid them both good-bye and keep working. After an hour I get up to buy myself a coffee, because even though I don't really have money, it goes against my code to mooch. I won't even use the bathroom at McDonalds without buying something.

But when I reach for money, Kyle waves it off. "I got it," he says. "We're glad to have you here."

Another hour, and it's closing time. I get up to go, and Kyle holds up a paper cup. "Hey, you want some coffee to go? I'm just going to dump it out otherwise."

He's got a deal.

Walking through the nippy air to my car, coffee cup in hand and laptop slung over my shoulder, I can't help reflecting on how wealthy I am. I don't really have a penny to my name, yet here I am drinking artisan coffee, walking through a beautiful old neighborhood past two-story brick homes toward the river that borders Windsor to the north, and climbing into my car which, against all odds, I've been able to continue paying for all this time. I drive past the Hampton on my way back to my parents'—where recently I had a private office on the seventeenth floor.

This year hasn't been anything I've wanted it to be—in some ways.

In other ways, it's been more than I could have asked for.

I've spent the better part of a year doing creative work. I've built an audience and a thriving blog; I've written two new books, I've broken through writer's block. I've created a course I'm proud of, even if it didn't really sell, and I've maybe helped change some people's lives. I've walked, prayed, and learned to see in ways I've never seen before. I've built up experience—something I realize, as I have never realized it before, that you can't shortcut. And that is tremendously valuable.

No matter what happens after this, I'm grateful for this year. I'm grateful for its challenges, its highs and lows, and how far I've come.

And I'm proud, too. Even if I've become the girl who can't afford a haircut or a pair of jeans that fit or a cup of coffee, who couldn't keep her promises to herself, who has to go crawling back to a job she thought she'd left behind, at least I've become that girl in pursuit of something worth doing.

I don't know what I'll be doing tomorrow. Probably not this, anymore. More than likely, this run at a full-time writing career is over.

But I'll always be glad I tried.

PART 4:
The View from This Side of the River

BLUEPRINTS

ON NEW YEAR'S DAY, 2018, I take my cue from an encouragement released by an Australian woman named Lana Vawser, who writes and releases "prophetic words" on Facebook. I discovered her early in 2017 through a recommendation from a reader, and—although I was initially skeptical at the very idea of prophesying via social media—her words have been so uncannily relevant for me all year long that I've long since stopped questioning that they come from God.

"The battle has been so long and hard," she says, "that many of you have lost hope. But now it's time to go back to Jesus, go back to the drawing board, and ask him for the blueprints for this year. Be open to its being different to what you thought. Take time to sit with him and ask for the blueprints going forward."

So I do.

I go into this "meeting" with Jesus expecting to hear that my dreams from last year were askew. That I was wrong to take the leaps I did, when I did; that I was wrong to think that I could support myself solely through my writing and ministry—that I was wrong, maybe, even to want that. I expect to hear a call to humble myself and accept the hard truth that I was wrong and that now I need to build back up from the ruins and let go of my fool's hopes for a miraculous turnaround.

That's a bitter pill to swallow, yes, but after all—I've already more than half swallowed it.

But when I sit down to pray and strategize, something unexpected happens: I experience a renewal of my soul.

I can't tell you how or why. All I know is that I go to pray with sad resignation and I come out with renewed, unreasonable hope.

I come out believing I wasn't wrong after all. That the fierceness of the battle does not reflect the foolishness but rather the value of the dream.

As I face the new year, I don't know how I will go on. I don't know how it will be possible to stay true, to pay the bills. But the fear … the fear is mostly gone. It is replaced by peace, by joy, by a victory on the inside. And by perspective.

Humility doesn't taste great at first, and as I tell this story, I really want to "spin" everything so I don't have to eat any mud. I don't want to admit I made some wrong decisions along the way, as I most assuredly did. I don't want to admit to having freaked out, lost my cool, dragged my feet, or fallen apart, but I did all that too.

But it's a funny thing: keep humility in your mouth for a moment and the taste changes. It becomes the sweetness of gratitude and of release—the peace of knowing that you are not capable of doing everything right all the time, and that it's in your wrongness and your weakness that trust in the faithfulness of God takes over.

I launch *Seeds* a week later than planned, mid- January. It doesn't do nearly as well as I hoped—certainly it doesn't raise $10,000, and it doesn't spell the end of my struggle by a long shot. But it does hit #1 on the Christian Fantasy charts, and it gets the best reviews of anything I've ever written. It hasn't made an overnight difference, and yet I know it is a picture of the future.

A week after releasing *Seeds*, I have surgery to remove the fibroid that has slowly dismantled my health for the last two years. It's the turnaround my body needs, and although yes, it's a surgery with long-term ramifications, I am deeply at peace about this too.

As I come to grips with the idea that my latest plan

to turn my finances around has failed at that goal, I spend time hurting in my heart and in my body as I recover from major surgery—but I'm conscious that this is the pain of healing. I find more online workshops that teach how to publish and market effectively, and I renew my commitment to writing, with a new crystallization around the idea that it's writing, actually writing and publishing books, that needs to stay at the forefront of what I do with my time and energy—not consulting, contracting, launching, making courses, checking email, or any of the other thousand things I could do day by day.

A month ago I would not have believed I could have so much hope, so much renewed direction, so much strength to go another step on this journey. But they say the journey changes you, and it's true. Faith changes you too—the process of trusting, day after difficult day, forms steel and sinew and strategic softness in your innermost being.

Given my own head, my own will, last year's story would have been straightforward. Start at Point A, progress directly to Point B. I would have chosen to do without the meandering, the feeling lost, the winding trails and barely-trails and non-trails. Like the Israelites, I followed the call of God into a tangle and took a left turn to the promised land.

As I write, I'm still trekking on that journey. One foot, word, and prayer in front of the other. I'm building experience. I'm building hope.

Romans 5:3–5 says it well:

> Not only so, but we also glory in our sufferings, because we know that suffering produces perseverance; perseverance, character; and character, hope. And hope does not put us to shame, because God's love has been poured out into our hearts through the Holy Spirit, who has been given to us. (Romans 5:3–5, NIV)

Was I wrong, at the beginning of this journey, when I heard God say I was crossing the border into the promised land? No, I don't believe I was. When I look around me, all I see is promise after promise, planted, growing, beginning to bloom. These promises will need tending and protecting. One day soon they will be ready to harvest.

Today as I put these words down on paper, I am no longer in crisis. I'm slowly moving forward. And I have been changed by the journey. I have faced many of my worst fears and come out the other side happier, more content, more in love with Jesus. I have seen God provide in ways that bewilder me (how is it that my bills were paid through all those months of little to no income and no vision or health to move forward?). I have embraced the call on my life and learned what really matters to me. I have seen chaff fall away and leave me raw and open, but more breathtakingly alive than I've ever been.

In this year of writing, business, and walking by faith, I have learned more about myself and my God than in any other season of my life, and I have done work I am proud of—work I know can change lives, work that is already doing so.

I have come through the wilderness. I have fought down giants. I am standing on my land, with a hoe and a scythe and a pen in my hand, and here I will remain till God tells me otherwise—tending to the writing, attending to the call.

This land—this writing life—is mine. It is a gift of God. And whatever battles still lie ahead, I will face them with the knowledge that he is with me, I am called, and he will help me.

To stay faithful.
To stay true.

EPILOGUE: BUSINESS NOTES COMPENDIUM

I LEARNED SOME THINGS in my year of marching through deserts, backtracked trails and all.

Nothing happens until we decide to get on the trail. My years of hobbyist publishing—avoiding the potential pains and challenges of actually trying to grow and go full-time—got me essentially nowhere. It was making the decision to step out and really do this thing, starting with buying a course to learn how and then opening my ConvertKit account, that truly changed things for me.

Clarity comes through process. I know beyond any shadow of a doubt what I am called to do. But I didn't when I started. It was taking the first steps, then the later ones, going the journey, that brought the clarity of calling into my life.

We need to believe we can learn. This is something

Eben Pagan says that has stuck with me. When we see others doing something we want to do, succeeding at it, meeting their goals, we need to believe those things are learnable. It's not just, *Can I do that?* (Usually we can't, not right out of the gate.) It's, *Can I learn to do it?*

This warning, of course: knowing something is not the same as doing it. I check and recheck myself, regularly, to make sure I'm actually taking action on the things I think I'm doing.

When it comes to the work you do, think first about the value you can add or create, and not about the money you can make. Money will follow work you're proud of, work that makes a difference. If this is turned around, you will lose passion and focus and be unable to truly enjoy the fruit of your labor.

Some goals just take a while. I mentioned the goal I set with Mercy and Carolyn of giving away 10,000 digital copies of *Fearless: Free in Christ in an Age of Anxiety*. Despite false starts, lags, and setbacks, we hit that goal roughly eighteen months later—shortly before this book went to press. At the moment *Fearless* is the best-selling of all my titles.

God calls us to prosper. It's important to know this, to not poor-mouth ourselves as his children. At the same, prosperity has many facets and many layers. Finances may not be the only, first, or primary place where it's seen. Biblical prosperity is shalom: holistic wellness and harmony in every part of our lives, starting with and flowing from the spirit in our relationship with God.

I still don't know entirely what it means that the Lord is "for the body," but in this last year I've been grateful to learn that my physical needs matter to the Lord and that stewardship of the body is important. Rest, relaxation, recreation—these are not things to be ashamed of. They are gifts to be enjoyed and even responsibilities as we care for our bodies, the first gifts we are given by God and the means by which we experience life.

I began my journey to full-time creative work with an expectation of prosperity and success. I have had both for a short season, and I have had hardship and struggle for a longer one. It turns out that I was not, primarily, invited to a journey of success. Instead I was invited to the adventure of growth. I have never been so conscious of my own transformation.

Whatever faith journey beckons you, you are invited to the same adventure.

RESOURCES

Courses I Took and Recommend for Anyone Who Wants to Make a Living as a Creative

—Intentional Blog by Jeff Goins

—Your First 10K Readers by Nick Stephenson

—Ads for Authors by Mark Dawson

—Product Launch Formula by Jeff Walker

—Free to Focus by Michael Hyatt

A Course I Did Not Take But I Do Recommend

—Instant Bestseller by Tim Grahl

Books I Recommend

—*Deep Work: Rules for Focused Success in a Distracted World* by Cal Newport

—*Essentialism: The Disciplined Pursuit of Less* by Greg McKeown

—*Tribes: We Need You to Lead Us* and *What to Do When It's Your Turn (And It's Always Your Turn)* by Seth Godin

And of course, I highly recommend my email service provider: ConvertKit.

ALSO BY RACHEL STARR THOMSON

FICTION

The Chronicles of Kepos Gé

Seeds: A Christian Fantasy

The Oneness Cycle

Exile

Hive

Renegade

Attack

Rise

The Prophet Trilogy

Abaddon's Eve

Comes the Dragon

Beloved

The Seventh World Trilogy

Worlds Unseen

Burning Light

Coming Day

STANDALONE NOVELS

Angel in the Woods

Lady Moon

Reap the Whirlwind

Taerith

The Babel Chip

The City Came Creeping

Theodore Pharris Saves the Universe

SHORT STORIES

Butterflies Dancing

Fallen Star

Journey

Magdalene

Of Men and Bones

Ogres Is

Shields of the Earth

War With the Muse

Wayfarer's Dream

NONFICTION

Heart to Heart: Meeting with God in the Lord's Prayer

Letters to a Samuel Generation: The Collection

Mind Soul Ink Paper and Other Essays on Faith, Reading, and Writing

Now for the Not-Yet and Other Essays on Everyday Discipleship

Still Praying in the Wilderness and Other Essays for the Spiritually Thirsty

Tales of the Heartily Homeschooled

Undivided Devotion

Your Kingdom Calling: 3 Keys to Discovering Your Calling and Purpose in the Kingdom of God

Fearless: Free in Christ in an Age of Anxiety (with Mercy Hope and Carolyn Currey)

Fifty Shades of Loved (with Mercy Hope, Kit Tosello, Katie Rees, Shea Wood, Susan Milligan, and Laura Leigh-Anne Busick)